Anonymous

Church Service in Outline

with chants and metrical hymns, for Congregational worship

Anonymous

Church Service in Outline
with chants and metrical hymns, for Congregational worship

ISBN/EAN: 9783337081812

Printed in Europe, USA, Canada, Australia, Japan

Cover: Foto ©Lupo / pixelio.de

More available books at **www.hansebooks.com**

Church Service,

IN OUTLINE:

WITH

Chants and Metrical Hymns,

FOR ⟨ ⟩ SHIP:

A ⟨ ⟩ ldar.

"If the parson were ashamed of particularizing in these things, he were not fit to be a parson. But he holds the rule, that nothing is little in God's service ; if it once have the honor of THAT NAME, it grows great instantly." THE COUNTRY PARSON.

NEW YORK:
BARNES & BURR, 51 & 53 JOHN ST.,
A. D. F. RANDOLPH, 683 BROADWAY.
1864.

PREFACE.

THERE is no careful observer of religious affairs, who does not know that in many of our great Christian Denominations, the methods of public worship are exciting an unaccustomed interest and inquiry. History, philosophy, devotion, are supplying, each its element, in this new discussion ; and many christian minds are inquiring—how and when did the present usages in worship arise — under what pressure of events or by what appointment of God ? — what foundation have they in the structure and laws of the human soul ? — how far do they help the Christian assembly to edify itself and honor the Most High in its acts of public devotion? — what is their present actual work in bringing to bear upon a heedless world the most direct and powerful pressure of Christ's Gospel ? Such inquiries, and a careful observation of present facts concerning public worship, have produced more or less dissatisfaction in many minds who yet remain in ignorance of the extent to which their own feeling is shared by others, and many of whom without method of action or even of thought upon this theme, are uneasily waiting for some indefinite improvements to be developed. The compiler of the Service here presented in outline, seeks not so much to awaken thought or guide opinion upon public worship, as to supply to thought already awakened, some one clear and definite system applicable to non-prelatical, and especially to Congregational churches,— which shall have at least a character and consistency of its own, and whose very faults, with the proper criticisms which they may excite, shall serve as the stepping-stones, or as the warnings, for other and better guides. Something is gained for the prevention of vagueness and aimlessness, by providing discussion with an object. The object itself may be of little worth, and its fate of no great moment ; and yet it may render essential service in the crystallization of opinion.

It will be idle for any to strive to preclude attempts at the improvement of public worship, by the old outcry against *forms*, and the danger which they involve. The common mind of the present day is sufficiently instructed to perceive that it is impossible for *any* public worship to exist without forms,— that even a supposed *lack of forms* is itself a form which may even claim for itself an almost saving grace, and assume a rigor and exclusiveness most destructive to spiritual life — and that therefore since forms are inevitable, it is well to study for the securing of those that shall minister the highest edification. Whatever may befall individual preferences, or present usages, or attempts at change, discussion will go on ; and in its freeness and fulness will lead, under God's good guidance, perhaps through repeated failures, to the ultimate success.

It is intended to present in this Pamphlet, as an experiment, a mere *outline* of a system of public Christian Services. Nothing is given with any approach to completeness except such musical selections as are in their arrangement peculiar to this Service. These are here printed for temporary use in a Congregational church* to which the compiler ministers as Pastor, and in which for more than a year past, this Service.

*The Bedford Church, Brooklyn, New York.

4

in an incomplete form, has been in use. It is not expected that this Pamphlet will gain any wide circulation outside the Parish for whose use it is especially prepared. But, a larger Book of Worship, developing the system here presented, is being prepared, and will in a few months be issued if it shall promise to meet any want, or to be practically helpful toward any improvement in conducting the public services of Christ's House

The music for the chants, and sentences here set forth, has been prepared and arranged by a skilful and accomplished musical composer. Mr. EDWARD WIEBE, of Brooklyn, and can be had separately, for the use of choirs, by application to the publishers of this Pamphlet.

VARIOUS PARTS OF SERVICE.

Public Divine Service comprises two departments — Worship and Instruction: the first, addressed to God; the second, to man. While it is not to be denied that all proper Divine Worship is instructive, nor that all proper Christian Instruction is worshipful, it is yet true that these two departments are rightfully to be distinguished from each other, in respect of the *methods* which are appropriate to them severally in practice. A just philosophy shows that variety, and even a startling novelty, are not misapplied, when by their aid Divine Instruction gains impressiveness upon the mind; and a philosophy equally just, shows that, in general, *Public Worship*, while needing a variety of form sufficient to avoid monotony, is not greatly aided by either studied or careless diversities, and depends but slightly on novelty for its force, and is even hindered and distracted by trains of thought or forms of words elaborately new and strange, and moves easiest toward God through paths that have been travelled so often as to have become familiar — the habitudes of the soul.

The plan of Public Services here presented, aims to recognize these principles, and others similar which will occur to any one who analyzes the laws of mental impression and moral emotion. Certain portions of the general department of Worship, including Prayer and Praise, are left to the impulse or inspiration of the moment; although this can be only partially true regarding Praise, since every hymn of praise is in its very nature a Liturgy, a written form of worship, which for the moment sets aside all the unpremeditated effusions of individual worshippers. Still, from a wide range of hymns, a selection can be made which shall be so special in its fitness to a case in hand, that it shall have a character almost extemporaneous. Then, certain other portions of Prayer and Praise, are arranged to recur in a regular order, weekly, monthly, annually; and are prepared with particular reference to those general wants which are present to every human soul worshipping before God; also the very element of familiarity, gained by such frequent recurrence, will be found to make it far more easy and natural for the whole assembly to join their voices in these acts of direct worship; without which audible participation, the spirit of Prayer and Praise, though it may indeed exist, certainly does not present itself in all its appropriate beauty before God's public altars, and does not go forth in all its proper power upon the hearts of men. To claim that the arrangement here attempted is the best that can be made for the purpose, would be to claim that a mere experiment is a success; but to assert that in *some such* way alone, can Congregational Singing and Praying become actual in the *generality* of our churches, is only to assert principles old and deep as man himself.

MUSICAL SERVICES.

These, as here provided, may, by a general classification which shall refer to both the words and the tunes, be arranged in the order of their simplicity and adaptability to public worship, under four heads.—

1.—*The Plain Chant*, scarcely more than Recitative ; a mere intoning or cantillating of words, which, like those of Holy Scripture, are without poetic rhyme or rhythm. This is sometimes known as the " Ancient Plain Song of the Church." It was undoubtedly the style of musical service in the time of the Apostles and of our Lord. If performed antiphonally or responsively, it re-produces the style in which, for ages, the Hebrew Psalms were chanted in the worship of God. It is the plainest possible music, differing least from the ordinary speaking voice ; and as uttered in the very words of Holy Scripture by a congregation of worshippers, is capable of a massive grandeur whose methods of simplicity and directness, hallowed as they are by the use of prophets, apostles, and the Lord Himself, the church can ill-afford altogether to spare for the sake of performing *all* its worship in the words of artistic odes, in which too often sentiment and devotion are sacrificed to rhyme and rhythm, while the music walks in the four-fold chain of an intricate scientific harmony. Rhymed hymns have their place, their merits, their uses, in public Christian Services ; but their excellence will not be hindered, but helped rather, by restoring to the House of Prayer, which is beautified by their more modern art, those sublime echoes of Zion's ancient songs which linger even yet where stood of old the Temple at Jerusalem, and the Upper Chamber, and the homes of the first churches of Jesus Christ. In view of such considerations as these, it is here arranged that in every Service a lesson from the Psalter shall be responsively cantillated (or *said*, if from any cause this be deemed preferable by a church) by the united voices of the congregation. This lesson, which is unlike the corresponding selection from the Psalter in the Protestant Episcopal Book of Common Prayer, in being taken from the common version of the Bible, and also in being much shorter,—is always immediately followed by a regular chant in the modern style, or by a hymn in metre and rhyme ; so that thus the church beginning her song with the simple ages past, completes it with the gifts of a later art, rising at the end to a Doxology higher than the Hebrew ever knew — an ascription to God as Father, Son, and Holy Ghost.

The Book of Psalms, from which are omitted some small portions unfitted for modern public worship, is apportioned to the various Calendar Days of the Year. This attempt to assign appropriate lessons from the Psalter to particular Days, is, doubtless, only a partial success, which it is to be hoped some wiser guide may improve. But no other arrangement which seemed preferable has yet presented itself. The arrangement for *daily* reading of the Psalter, thus completing the Book monthly, which undoubtedly proves edifying in the Service of the Protestant Episcopal Church, is, because of the length of the lessons, and for other reasons, unsuited to the congregations for which this experiment is made. Attention is invited to the fact that the *divisions* for the responsive reading of the Psalms, are not, as in many Services, made to agree with the old Monkish, unauthorized, and, often absurd division into *verses* in our English Bible ; but mainly re-produce the still older and natural division which is demanded by the very structure of the Psalms themselves, and which alone preserves that simple and beautiful Parallelism that prominently characterizes the Hebrew poetry. By this arrangement —one member of the Parallelism recited by one voice or set of voices, and the other member by the responsive voices — not only are the Psalms presented in their natural and primitive style, but a fuller and more reverent unison of utterance is secured than when long sentences are rapidly recited by the voices of a multitude.*

2.—*The Common Chant*, single or double, more or less developed in *harmony* for the organ and choir, but retaining a simple *unison* for the voices of the congregation. In structure this stands next in simplicity to the cantillated Psalm. It has the same lack of rhyme and rhythm, and is also in the words of Holy Scripture, and thus is less dependent on art than is a hymn in metre. Though perhaps to some modern choirs, not easy of execution because of the disuse into which it may have fallen, it is nevertheless in its own structure simple and well adapted to be the channel of general worship. As here arranged, the same chants (words and music) recur at regular intervals— five being assigned to the Mornings and five to the Evenings of the Lord's Days in each month. This secures familiarity and facility of performance, those efficient helps to direct congregational Praise. This monthly order is interrupted (if the Calendar be used as recommended) by chants provided for special days like the Nativity, or the Ascension, and which on such appointed days take the place of the regular monthly chant; thus through an impressive fitness to the day, introducing a perhaps needful variety in the Service. These special chants however, being the same year by year, will steadily accumulate value and force by use. The regular order in which these chants recur, enables them to be sung without announcement, as though they were the spontaneous uprising of all hearts to God. Much care has been taken in the selection of the words for these Biblical songs. These are not, like many of the chants in constant use in various Denominations, and suited doubtless to the work there assigned them, mere introductions or invitations to Praise, or pious reflections about Praise — " O come, let us sing ! " — "It is a good thing to give thanks," etc. — but they are, at least in large portions, Praise itself in expressions direct from the singer to God.

In this class may be ranked also *The Great Doxology*, or "*Gloria In Excelsis*," — a sublime song combining humble supplication with confession of faith and ascription of praise, whose origin is traced to a period only thirty or forty years later than the Apostolic. Of all uninspired hymns, this and the " *Te Deum* " are the noblest and the grandest. *The Great Doxology* is arranged to be sung by all at every Morning Service on the Lord's Day, in an irregular but ancient and simple chant.

The Less Doxology, or " *Gloria Patri* " closes every chant.

3.—*The Metrical Hymn in Rhyme*. This familiar form of sacred song has a strong hold on the popular regard, and in its best estate possesses many excellences. As here arranged, it supplies about one half of all the musical Services for Morning and Evening. A distinction is recognized between hymns sung by the assembly to God, and hymns sung by the choir to the assembly. The former belong under the head of Worship ; the latter under the head of Instruction. A vast number of our modern hymns are addressed to men, viewed as Christians or the opposite ; they are not worship ; they are sermons more than praises. It is proper that these should be used ; the choir may preach as well as the minister.— often better ; but this musical preaching should not be called *Praise*. It admits of novelty, and scientific effort, and elaborate structure, both in words and tune ; — solo, duet, trio, quartette, all are in place here.

---

*In this Pamphlet, containing only the outline of the Service, it is necessary to omit entirely the selections from the Psalter referred to above. Examples of the contemplated arrangement may be seen in the *chants* for regular Morning and Evening Service on the Lord's Day, in which the alternate lines mark the divisions which would be used for responsive reading.

This class of singing has great effect at the close of a sermon whose instructions it prolongs and repeats with delicate musical echoes. *One* Metrical Hymn, however, in each Service, is by the arrangement now contemplated, secured for direct Praise. By an assignment corresponding to that of the chants above noted, the same hymns recur in a monthly order, set aside on the special Calendar Days (The Nativity, The Ascension, etc.) for special hymns fitted to the fact or sentiment which the day expresses. These familiar monthly or annual hymns, sung always each in its own peculiar tune, in unison of all the voices of the assembly, without formal announcement from the pulpit, and completed as all hymns intended for *Praise* should complete themselves, in the Doxology to God as Father, Son, and Holy Ghost, are expected to procure by their familiarity and simplicity, true congregational singing. so much praised and desired, so little practically attained.

4.—*The Anthem.* This may be considered the most elaborate style of christian song. It admits of a high degree of intricacy in its musical composition, and generally demands artistic culture and skill in its performance. Yet it may well comprise choruses in which at intervals the voices of the congregation bursting forth in unison. may produce magnificent effect, expressing worship and enforcing truth. But the remoteness of its general style from the grand simplicity that should ordinarily characterize worship. renders it undesirable as a *constant* feature in the services of Christian song. In the system as here presented, therefore, it is provided that occasionally, at the discretion of those (such as minister, choir-master) who direct the music, an anthem may take the place of the metrical hymn before the sermon in Evening Service. Thus its use may be sufficiently frequent to supply the choir with the needful opportunity and inducement for high musical culture, and yet not so frequent as to give the musical service in general an aspect so elaborate and artistic as shall remove it from the sympathies of the mass of worshippers. Brief anthems, however, in the form of responsive introductions. whose brevity as also their position in the Service prevent their interfering with the general directness of worship, are also provided, with a view to elevating the minds of the assembly and summoning their attention. and disposing their thoughts for the worship in which they have come to engage.

The " Te Deum " also may be noted under this head, as it is here arranged to be sung as an introductory anthem at the celebration of the Lord's Supper. Its character as a Hymn of High Praise has given it a place also in the Services of The Nativity, The Ascension. and Thanksgiving Day. Recurring thus eight or ten times in the year, it soon becomes familiar in words and music to the worshipping assembly, whose voices may join in the portions assigned as choruses, swelling thus the volume of Christian song that has now, since the early centuries of the Gospel, echoed through the sanctuaries of God's saints. For the " Te Deum," which is one of the most ancient Christian hymns, has been well described as " at once the most noble Song of Thanksgiving, the most sublime Confession of Faith, and the most animated Supplication for Pardon and Grace, to be found among the devotional treasures of the Christian World."

.

THE ORDER OF SERVICES.

The Service here presented in outline is recommended by the fact that its material is *not new*, except in portions of slight importance or extent. Its verbal forms are mostly venerable with age. They are majestic in the very words of Holy Scripture; or august with an almost Apostolic usage; or rich with the quick emotions of oriental climes; or simple with the childlikeness of the primitive faith: or dignified with a catholic use in the days when purity was catholic; or stalwart with the manliness and fervent with the zeal of the German and English Reformers. And as the Formulas mostly are ancient, so their arrangement in this Order of Service is not new. The logical structure of the ancient Presbyterian Liturgies by Calvin and other Reformers — a structure commended by its simplicity, massiveness, comprehensiveness, and especially by its natural gradations — has been generally taken as the model for the Morning Service; while yet the logical procession of parts has been slightly compromised for the sake of that variety which seems in our times indispensable to edification. Only one such logical and complete Service however is needful in one day: therefore the Evening Service, by which is intended any Service after noon-day whether before or after sun-set, is fashioned (though quite remotely) on a different, yet ancient model — that of the almost primitive Vespers, whose character, as musical, scriptural and responsive, so fitted to the day's decline, and so sweetly contrasted with the sterner and broader Morning worship, has already caused its re-appearance in Protestant usage.

The procession of parts in the *Morning Service* may be thus described.—The Service opens with tones from the *Organ*, subduing the rustle of the assembly and calming and exalting the soul in preparation for Divine Worship. As the Organ ceases, a brief *Sentence* of Holy Scripture uttered by the Minister turns the thought directly to God, His Day, His Sanctuary, His Truth, His Majesty, or His Worship. To this succeeds a musical *Response* of similar character and impression, which serves still further to summon attention and to set forth the responsive and united nature of the Service now entered upon — heart answering heart, and voice echoing voice:— If not sung, this response may be *said* by the congregation. At this point, the universal and inevitable fact of sinfulness, meets the worshipper, whose rightful impulse it is first of all to confess and forsake his transgressions. The Service aiming to imitate the work of God's truth upon the heart, which bases itself always on the fact of sin and therefrom develops all high attainments, introduces here the *Law of God*, uttered by the Minister while all reverently stand: which Law leads to proper views of sin, and prepares the congregation to kneel in humble *Confession* before the Most High. This General Confession including prayer for pardon and a renewed dedication, fitly passes into a General *Profession of Christian Faith*, in which act, the congregation still further establishing themselves in this Grace wherein they stand, rise and proceed to declare with united voice in the words of the *Apostles' creed*, the grand and simple essentials of the Gospel. Then the Minister utters the *Comforting Words* of God's Grace in the Gospel to those who have humbly confessed their sins under the Law; immediately after which the congregation appropriately lift up their voices in the *Great Doxology*, or " *Gloria In Excelsis*." General Petitions and Intercessions (the longest Prayer) here follow — Intercession being the loftiest and most Christ-like act of worship. These prayers may be, at the discretion of the Minister, either the Ancient *Litany*, or short detached forms previously composed, or, entirely extemporaneous. At the close, a moment's *Silence* is devoted to the secret out-pouring of each separate heart to God; and this silence is broken by the *Lord's Prayer*, which as a comprehensive summary of all possible requests, completes the act of Prayer. The congregation then rise, and praise God in the responsive singing or reading of the *Psalter* for the Day, which is instantly succeeded by the *Metrical Hymn of Praise* for the Day, which in turn completes itself with the *Doxology* to God as Father, Son, and Holy Ghost. Immediately then, the *Offertory*, or charitable contribution, has its place on such days as are appointed; and this is of the nature of Devotion, and takes rank with prayer and praise; since those who have interceded before God for others, and have rendered praise for all His mercies to themselves, are strictly bound to show the sincerity of such pious words, in their gifts for the unfortunate, according to their ability. Any needful and proper *Notices* may here be given; and then the *Lessons of Holy Scripture* as assigned for the Day, are read by the Minister; after which all join in the *Chant* for the Day ending with "*Gloria Patri*". Divine Instruction then proceeds in the form of a *Sermon*; and of a *Closing Hymn* in Metre, which not being necessarily worship, but often the echo of the Sermon — *need* not be sung by all, but *may* generally be performed by the Choir, as the other more worshipful music should seldom be. The congregation then kneel in a closing *Prayer*, including *Benediction*, pronounced by the Minister; and after a few seconds of reverent silence, the Organ sounds, the worshippers rise, and disperse; and the Service is ended.

GENERAL REMARKS.

The liberty which this Service allows is noticeable. It aims to impose no forms of prayer except the formula which our Lord has given. Other forms are offered simply as helps, to be used or set aside at pleasure; though indeed it is strongly recommended that the *General Confession*, in parts of which the congregation are expected to join, shall be usually in the words which the Service provides. But the longest Prayer is left free — being supplied with ancient and beautiful forms, which *may* or *may not* be used, as circumstances may dictate. The Introductory Response *may* give place to a different musical selection; and the Metrical Hymn for the Day also may be set aside for any similar hymn that shall seem more appropriate; though this last change certainly is not recommended. Also, instead of the hymn before Sermon in Evening Service, an Anthem may occasionally be introduced.

The use of the Calendar with its Offices for the Christian Year, may also be various. If any Church choose to omit all the special Days there remains the *monthly* order of Chants, Hymns, etc. If any choose to observe only the five great Church Days, they can omit all the others without confusion.

The Compiler, far from claiming originality for this Service, deems its chief merit to consist in the fact that it is a compilation from many and diverse sources, in which sense it may be reckoned at least, a tribute, if not a help, to Christian unity. In its preparation, he has been aided by those two scholarly and instructive works, "A Book of Public Prayer," and "Eutaxia, or the Presbyterian Liturgies." "The Book of Common Prayer" comprising the Services of the Protestant Episcopal Church, than which there exists no Devotional manual richer and more complete, — and "Christian Worship," comprising the tasteful Services recently set forth for the use of Unitarian Christians, — have each supplied material or suggestion. Essential aid has been derived also from the experimental " Liturgy of the German Reformed Church "; and the more ancient and almost Apostolic formulas, such as the Greek Liturgy of St. James, or of Antioch, in the Rev. Dr. F. H. Hedge's translation, have not been overlooked. Acknowledgments for some of the Metrical Hymns of Worship, are due to the Publishers respectively of "Songs of the Church," and of "The Sabbath Hymn Book" — to the latter especially for four Metrical Hymns in the " Offices for Special Days," as follows:— Mid Winter Day, &c., Evening, "*Hope of our Hearts, O Lord! appear*": — The Crucifixion Day, &c., Morning, "*Thou art the Everlasting Son*"; and Evening, "*O Christ our King, Creator, Lord!*":—The Ascension Day, &c., Evening, "*Lift up your heads, Ye Gates.*"

The whole Service can be regarded only as an experiment. Let its faults be corrected; let its excellences be adopted and retained fearlessly and in despite of prejudice; let other, abler, hands supply nobler and more fruitful offerings to the treasury of our common Christian worship; till the services of God's House shall come to stand in tender beauty and in massive strength, and in all the Grace and Presence of the Lord Himself, to Whom, be Glory in the Church, forevermore!

THE CHURCH CALENDAR.

All the days of a Christian's life are consecrated to God. No one day therefore is to be held in superstitious regard. Yet the Ordinance of God, as uttered both in His constitution of the human soul, and in His express Revelation, show the benefit of assigning special days to special thoughts of Devotion. The Jewish Church, at the Divine command, kept its annual and its weekly Sabbaths: and these, though duly transfigured by the Gospel, have never been abrogated. The ancient Sabbath, enriched with new meaning by Christ's victorious Resurrection, and correspondingly changed in its period, became the LORD'S DAY; and the same pious sentiment which, with no recorded Divine command, led the first Christians to seek by such new use of the chief Hebrew Day to commemorate the Resurrection of the Lord, may properly lead us, as it undoubtedly led them, to set forth by the use of other days, the other grand facts of His Messiahship. Yet the Lord's Day, as having been in substance specially ordained of God from the Beginning, is through all Time to be held, chief of Days, in the Christian Church.

The minor facts of the historic Gospel, the lives of the Apostles, and the virtues of saints, whether of the Roman, or the Puritan communion, may safely be regarded as out of place in the Calendar of the Christian Church. Their commemoration, though to some minds possibly beneficial, is certainly burdensome by reason of number, and hazardous in its lifting of the non-essential in the Gospel to rank with the essential— of the human saint-ship with the Divine Messiahship.

The Calendar which sets forth the grand facts of the historic Gospel, will therein set forth also the prominent features of the individual and general human estate and experience. By an evident symbolism, the same Twelve-Month may be used also to figure God's Providence in the course of a human life from infancy to old age, and also in the progress of the seasons of the natural Year. Any of these minor applications of the Calendar may however be omitted without detriment to the main design.

THE CHRISTIAN SEASONS.

In the Calendar here presented, the Christian Year opens at about December 1st, and progresses through Four Seasons. Each of these Seasons marks an epoch in the historic development of the Gospel; and corresponds in general with one of the seasons of the natural Year; and figures a period in the life of man from infancy to age. Other applications, also, less important, are included. The various applications will appear on consulting the Calendar.

Each Season begins with a Lord's Day, and ends with a Saturday.

THE CALENDAR DAYS.

These include all Lord's Days, and all other commemorative Days, throughout the year. They are named and numbered in the Calendar, which embraces all of such Days that can possibly occur through an indefinite series of years; and thus, more than can ever occur in *any one* year. From the Calendar therefore, various days noted for that purpose are, in each year, omitted.

All the commemorative Days, except ordinary Lord's Days, are known as *Special Days*. Among these are the *five Great Church Days,— Nativity, Crucifixion, Resurrection, Ascension, Pentecost;* and the *two Great Civil Days,— Fast* and *Thanksgiving*. It is specially desirable that public Divine Service be held on these *seven Great Days*, of which two, and in some years, three, are Lord's Days.

The Lord's Days are held to begin at sunset on the Saturday previous. [Gen. I, 5.] This is not necessarily with a view to religious observance, which it is probably in vain now to attempt, but merely for the purpose of systematic arrangement in the Calendar.

Thursdays, in memory of the Lord's Ascension, are appropriate for any Festivals or joyous occasions.

Fridays, in memory of the Lord's Crucifixion, are appropriate for any Fasts, or penitential occasions.

All days not named in the Calendar, such as the usual *week days*, are held to repeat the sentiment, and to follow the rules of the last preceding Calendar-Day.

A Daily church service, if brief and simple, is certainly admissible and edifying, and may in some cases be practicable.

THE SACRAMENTS.

The Lord's Supper, with the service of Baptism or Introduction to Membership, is assigned to Eight occasions during the year — that at least as often as once at the beginning and once near the middle of each of the four seasons, the Church may comfort and enliven itself in Christ's Sacrament of the Supper, and publicly invite wandering hearts to *enter its communion* by Christ's Sacrament of Baptism. Yet, it should be understood that in addition to any fixed periods, the Church has, at all times, liberty for the observance of these Sacraments, imitating, if desirable, the unquestioned frequency of Apostolic usage.

The Baptism of Children is assigned to Four occasions during the year — that at least as often as once in each of the seasons, Parents may be officially reminded of their privilege and duty in this regard. Yet it should be understood that the Church is at all times ready to receive in Christ's Ordinance of Baptism all offerings of Children by their Parents or Guardians.

Calendar.

In these Tables, all the *Special Days* begin at the extreme left; and the Ordinary Lord's Days a little to the right. The occurrence of the Lord's Supper is marked by an asterisk—the Baptism of Children, by the sign †.

The first Messiaship, and final Coming of our Lord.—The world's early Winter of sin and need.—The original Winter of the Soul, amid which our Lord comes in His Grace.

I. Advent Season. [WINTER.]

Begins—Lord's Day Fourth before Nativity.
Comprises—Thirteen or Fourteen Lord's Days.
Ends—Saturday Next before Lord's Day Tenth after Nativity.

Cal. No.	Calendar Days	Limits	Occurrence, &c.	Significance
1	*Lord's Day First in Advent	Nov. 27—Dec. 3	L. D. 4th bef. Nativ.; or next after Thurs. last in Nov.	The world's early need and expectation of Messiah:—Second and final coming of our Lord:—Old age.
2	Lord's Day Second in Advent	Dec. 4—10		
3	Lord's Day Third in Advent	Dec. 11—17		
4	Lord's Day Fourth in Advent	Dec. 18—24	Yields, Dec. 24 (evg.), to No. 5	
5	The Nativity Eve	Dec. 24 (Evg.)		
6	The Nativity Day (*Christmas*)	Dec. 25		The Nativity of our Lord:—Human infancy.
7	*Lord's Day Next after Nativity	Dec. 26—31	Yields, Dec. 31 (evg.), to No. 8	
8	New Year Eve	Dec. 31 (Evg.)		Close of the Year
9	New Year Day	Jan. 1		
10	†New Year Lord's Day	Jan. 1—7	Yields, when L. D. to No. 10	Beginning of the Year, and of a Christian life.
11	Lord's Day Second after Nativity	Jan. 8		
12	Lord's Day Third after Nativity	Jan. 9—12		
13	Mid Winter Day	Jan. 16	May be preceded by No.14.—Yields when L. D. to No. 14	
14	Mid Winter Lord's Day	Jan. 13—19	L. D. on or nearest Jan. 16	Mid winter:—middle life:—midst of sorrows or sins.
15	Lord's Day Fourth after Nativity	Jan. 20—22		
16	Lord's Day Fifth after Nativity	Jan. 23—29		
17	Lord's Day Sixth after Nativity	Jan. 30—Feb. 5		
18	Lord's Day Seventh after Nativity	Feb. 6—12		
19	Lord's Day Eighth after Nativity	Feb. 13—19		
20	Lord's Day Ninth after Nativity	Feb. 20—26		

The Sacrificial character and work of our Lord.—The World's Spring-time of hope through the Gospel.—The Soul's Spring-time of Christian life.—Childhood and Youth.

Calendar.

II.
Paschal Season.
[SPRING.]

Begins—Lord's Day Tenth after Nativity.
Comprises—Ten, to Fifteen, Lord's Days.
Ends—Saturday Next before Pentecost.

Cal. No.	Calendar Days	Limits	Occurrence, &c.	Significance
21	*LORD'S DAY FIRST IN PASCHAL SEASON	Feb. 27—Mar. 5	L. D. 10th aft. Nativ.; 3d to 5th bef. Resur.	Promise of Spring:—Childhood
22	LORD'S DAY SECOND IN PASCHAL SEASON	Mar. 5—12	L. D. 2d to 7th bef. Resur.	
23	LORD'S DAY THIRD IN PASCHAL SEASON	Mar. 12—Ap. 11	From one to all of these five Lord's Days may need to be omitted in various years.—The largest numbers yield first.	
24	LORD'S DAY FOURTH IN PASCHAL SEASON	Mar. 19—Ap. 11		
25	LORD'S DAY FIFTH IN PASCHAL SEASON	Mar. 26—Ap. 11		
26	LORD'S DAY SIXTH IN PASCHAL SEASON	Ap. 2—11		
27	LORD'S DAY SEVENTH IN PASCHAL SEASON	Ap. 9—11		
28	CIVIL FAST DAY	Mar. 13—Ap. 16	Friday Next bef. Crucifixion; or, any day appointed by Civil Power	Public and National sins and Duties
29	LORD'S DAY NEXT BEFORE CRUCIFIXION	Mar. 15—Ap. 18		Institution of the Lord's Supper:—
30	The Crucifixion Eve	Mar. 19—Ap. 22	Thurs. (evg.) next bef. Crucif.	Agony in Gethsemane
31	The Crucifixion Day (Good Friday)	Mar. 20—Ap. 23	Fri. next bef. Resur.	Cross and Passion of our Lord
32	The Sepulchre Day.—The Resurrection Eve	Mar. 21—Ap. 24	Sat. next bef. Resur.:—The Resur. Eve begins at sunset	Death and Burial of our Lord
33	*The Resurrection Day (Easter)	Mar. 22—Ap. 25	L. D. 1st aft. full moon occurring on or next aft. Mar. 21	Resurrection of our Lord:—The General Resurrection:—Arrival of Spring:—Youth:—Christian growth
34	LORD'S DAY NEXT AFTER RESURRECTION	Mar. 29—May 2		
35	LORD'S DAY SECOND AFTER RESURRECTION	Ap. 5—May 9		
36	LORD'S DAY THIRD AFTER RESURRECTION	Ap. 12—May 16		
37	LORD'S DAY FOURTH AFTER RESURRECTION	Ap. 19—May 23		
38	LORD'S DAY NEXT BEFORE ASCENSION	Ap. 26—May 30	L. D. 5th aft. Resur.	
39	The Ascension Eve	Ap. 29—June 2	Day 39th (Wed. 6th) (evg.) aft. Resur.	
40	The Ascension Day	Ap. 30—June 3	Day 40th (Thurs. 6th) aft. Resur.	Ascension of our Lord:—Complete triumph of truth and goodness:—The Heavenly Glory
41	LORD'S DAY NEXT AFTER ASCENSION	May 3—June 6	L. D. 6th aft. Resur.	

Calendar.

III.

Pentecost Season.

[SUMMER.]

Begins—The Pentecost Eve.
Comprises—Fourteen, to Nineteen, Lord's Days.
Ends—Saturday Next before Autumnal Equinox (Sep. 23).

The Giving of the Holy Ghost.—The World's Summer in the proclamation of the Gospel, and in the establishment, enlargement, and edification of the Church.—The Soul's Summer through the Spirit of God.—Mature Christian experience. —Middle life.

Cal. No.	Calendar Days	Limits	Occurrence, &c.	Significance
42	The Pentecost Eve			
43	*The Pentecost Day (Whitsunday)	May 9—Jun. 12	Day 49th (Sat. 7th) (Eve.) aft. Resur.	Giving of the Holy Ghost
44	†Lord's Day Next after Pentecost	May 10—Jun.13	Day 50th (L. D. 7th) aft. Resur.	
45	Lord's Day Second after Pentecost	May 17—Jun.20		
46	Lord's Day Third after Pentecost	May 24—Jun.27		
47	Mid Year Day	May 31—Jun.30		
48	MID YEAR LORD'S DAY	Jul. 1	Yields, when L. D., to No. 48	Middle life:—Midst of business and cares
49	Lord's Day Fourth after Pentecost	Jul. 1—7	L. D. 1st in July	
50	Lord's Day Fifth after Pentecost	Jun.7—30...Jul. 4–11		
51	Mid Summer Day	Jun.11—30...Jul.1—12		
52	*MID SUMMER LORD'S DAY	Jul. 16	May be preceded by No.52.—Yields, when L. D., to No. 52	Noon of life:—Mature age:—Prosperity
53	Lord's Day Sixth after Pentecost	Jul. 13—19	L. D. on. or nearest, Jul. 16	
54	Lord's Day Seventh after Pentecost	Jun. 21—30...Jul. 3— 13...Jul. 20—25		
55	Lord's Day Eighth after Pentecost	Jun. 24—30...Jul. 3— 13...Jul. 20—Aug.1		
56	Lord's Day Eighth after Pentecost	Jul. 4—12...Jul. 20— Aug.8		
57	Lord's Day Ninth after Pentecost	Jul. 12...Jul. 20— Aug.15		
58	Lord's Day Tenth after Pentecost	Jul. 20—Aug. 22		
59	Lord's Day Eleventh after Pentecost	Jul. 26—Aug. 29		
60	Lord's Day Twelfth after Pentecost	Aug. 2—Sep. 5		
61	Lord's Day Thirteenth after Pentecost	Aug. 9—Sep 12		From one to all of these five Lord's Days may need to be omitted in various years. The largest numbers yield first.
62	Lord's Day Fourteenth after Pentecost	Aug.16—Sep.16		
63	Lord's Day Fifteenth after Pentecost	Aug.23—Sep.16		
64	Lord's Day Sixteenth after Pentecost	Aug.30—Sep. 16		
65	Lord's Day Seventeenth after Pentecost	Sep. 6—16		
65	Lord's Day Eighteenth after Pentecost	Sep. 13—16		

Calendar.

IV.
Church Season.
[AUTUMN.]

Begins—Lord's Day on, or Next before, Autumnal Equinox (Sep. 23).
Comprises—Ten, or Eleven, Lord's Days.
Ends—Saturday Next after Thursday Last in November.

The spread and triumph of the Church.—The ingathering of the moral harvest of the World in the last days.—Consummate Christian experience.—Later years of life.

Cal. No.	Calendar Days	Limits	Occurrence, &c.	Significance
66	*Lord's Day First in Church Season	Sep. 17—23	L. D. on, or Next bef., Sep. 23	Harvest time:—Beginning of Autumn
67	†Lord's Day Second in Church Season	Sep. 24—30		
68	Lord's Day Third in Church Season	Oct. 1—7		
69	Lord's Day Fourth in Church Season	Oct. 8—14		
70	Lord's Day Fifth in Church Season	Oct. 15—21		
71	*Lord's Day Sixth in Church Season	Oct. 22—28	L. D. 3d, or 4th, in Oct.	
72	Lord's Day Seventh in Church Season	Oct. 29—Nov. 4		
73	Lord's Day Eighth in Church Season	Nov. 5—11		
74	Lord's Day Ninth in Church Season	Nov. 12—18		
75	Lord's Day Tenth in Church Season	Nov. 19—25		
76	Lord's Day Eleventh in Church Season	Nov. 26		
77	CIVIL THANKSGIVING DAY	Nov. 24—30	Thurs. Last in Nov.; or, any day appointed by Civil Power	Public and National blessings and duties

The Principal Movable Calendar Days;

ALSO, THE NUMBERS OF LORD'S DAYS IN THE DIFFERENT SEASONS:

FOR A PERIOD OF SIX YEARS.

The asterisk marks the Days on which occurs the Lord's Supper.

Cal. No.	Days, &c.	1863-4	1864-5	1865-6	1866-7	1867-8	1868-9
		1863	1864	1865	1866	1867	1868
1	*Lord's Day First in Advent	Nov.29	Nov.27	Dec.3	Dec 2	Dec.1	Nov 29
6, or 7	*Lords Day on or next after the Nativity	Dec. 27	Dec 25	Dec.31	Dec. 30	Dec 29	Dec. 27
		1864	1865	1866	1867	1868	1869
10	NEW YEAR LORD'S DAY	Jan.3	Jan. 1	Jan 7	Jan 6.	Jan. 5	Jan. 3
14	MID WINTER LORD'S DAY	Jan. 17	Jan. 15	Jan. 14	Jan. 13	Jan. 19	Jan. 17
—	Total No. of Lord's Days in Advent Season	13	14	13	13	13	13
21	*Lord's Day First in Paschal Seas.	Feb. 28	Mar. 5	Mar.4	Mar.3	Mar.1	Feb. 28
—	No. of Lord's Days in Paschal Season before Resurrection	4	5	4	7	6	4
28	CIVIL FAST DAY [unless differently ordered by Civil Power]	Mar.18	Apr.7	Mar.23	Apr.12	Apr.3	Mar.19
31	The Crucifixion Day	Mar. 25	Apr. 14	Mar.30	Apr.19	Apr.10	Mar.26
33	*The Resurrection Day	Mar.27	Apr 16	Apr.1	Apr.21	Apr.12	Mar.28
40	The Ascension Day	May 5	May 25	May 10	May 30	May 21	May 6
—	Total No. of Lord's Days in Paschal Season	11	12	11	14	13	11
43	*The Pentecost Day	May 15	June 4	May 20	June 9	May 31	May 16
48	MID YEAR LORD'S DAY	July 3	July 2	July 1	July 7	July 5	July 4
52	*MIDSUMMER LORDS DAY	July 17	July 16	July 15	July 14	July 19	July 18
—	No. of Lord's Days after Pentecost	17	14	17	14	15	17
—	Total No. of Lord's Days in Pentecost Season	18	15	18	15	16	18
66	*Lord's Day First in Church Seas.	Sep. 18	Sep. 17	Sep. 23	Sep. 22	Sep. 20	Sep. 19
71	*Lord's Day Sixth in Church Seas.	Oct. 23	Oct. 22	Oct. 28	Oct. 27	Oct. 25	Oct. 24
77	CIVIL THANKSGIVING DAY [unless differently ordered by Civil Power]	Nov.24	Nov.30	Nov.29	Nov.28	Nov.26	Nov.25
—	Total No. of Lord's Days in Church Season	10	11	10	10	10	10

Introductories.

FOR MORNING OR EVENING SERVICE.

————•◆•————

One or more of these portions of Holy Scripture, pronounced by Minister.

(In the book to be issued, more than one hundred of these are provided, to be printed in full.)

II Jn, 3.
Gal. i, 3, 4, 5.
II Pet. i, 2, 3.
Lam. iii, 40, 41. ,
Ps. xxvii. 14.
Ps. xcix, 9
Ps. cv, 4.
Ps. cxvii.
Ps. cxxxv, 2. 3.
Ps. cxxx, 7, 8.
Ps. xxxiii, 8, 9.
Ps. cxlvi, 10.
Ps. xx. 1, 2.
Is. lix. 1.
Rev. xix, 5. part.
Ps. xcvii, 1, 2.
Ps. cxxi, 1, 2.
Mic. vii. 7, part.
Ps. xxxiii, 20, 21, 22.
Ps. cxxiv, 8.
Is. lvii, 15, part.
Ps. lxxii, 18, 19.
Ps. ciii, 1. 2.
Ps. cxlv, 18, 19.
Is. xxv, 1.
Ps. xxii, 3, part.
Rev. xix, 6, part.
Rev. xv, 4.
Rev. iv, 11.
Ps. xxi, 13.
Ps. ix, 1, 2.
Ps. xxix, 4, 10.
Ps. xix, 14
Ps, lxv, 1, 2.
Ps. viii, 1.
Ps. xxxvi, 7, 9.

Ps. xlviii, 10.
Ps. xciii, 4. 5.
Ps. xcii, 1, 2.
Ps. cxlv, 3, 4.
Hos. vi, 3.
Lam. iii, 25, 26.
Is. lxii, 11.
Jas. iv, 8, 10.
Is. xxvi, 8. part.
Rev. v, 13, part.
I Tim. iii, 16, part.
II Cor. iv, 6, part.
Is. xii, 2, 3.
Is. lii, 10.
Jn. iv, 23, 24, part.
Ps. lxviii, 35.
Is. lxvi, 1.
Is. ii, 3, part.
Rev. xxi, 3, part.
Ps. xxii, 28, part.
Ps. xlvi. 4.
Ps. xlviii, 1.
Ps. xlviii, 2, 3.
Ps. xlviii, 12, 13, 14.
Hab. ii, 20, part.
Ps. lxiii, 1, 2.
Ps. cxlix, 4.
Ps. xx.
Ps. lxvii.
Ps. xciii.
Ps. c.
Ps cxxi.
Ps. cxxvi.
Ps. cxxx.
Ps cxxxiii.
Ps. cl.

For Evening Service, alone :—Ps. cxxxiv. Ps. cxli, 1, 2.

18

Lord's Day.—Morning Service.

ORDER.

I. Organ Voluntary.

II. { Introductory:—
Response.

III. The Law.

IV. General Confession.

V. Profession of Faith.

VI. Declaration of Grace.

VII. The Great Doxology—"*Gloria In Excelsis.*"

VIII. General Prayer; *ending with* "*The Lord's Prayer.*"

IX. The Matin Psalm (*Psalter for the Day*).

X. The Metrical Hymn of Worship.

XI. Offertory (*when appointed*).

XII. Notices (*when needful*).

XIII. The Lessons of Holy Scripture.

XIV. The Chant.

XV. Sermon.

XVI. Metrical Hymn.

XVII. { Prayer:—
Benediction.

XVIII. Organ Voluntary.

When the Sacrament of Baptism, or the Service of Introduction to Membership, is observed, that Special Service takes the place of V, VI.

When the Lord's Supper is observed, its Special Service takes the place of XV, XVI, XVII, XVIII.—But XV is, if desirable, retained in a much shortened form.

Lord's Day.

MORNING SERVICE.

I. ORGAN VOLUNTARY.—

Beginning as Minister enters — not earlier than five minutes before the time appointed for Service :

Ending, three minutes after the time.—

II. INTRODUCTION.—

[All stand.]

1.—Minister pronounces one or more of the portions of Holy Scripture set forth as *Introductories ;* or the portion set forth below, which the Choir are about to sing.—

2.—Choir or Congregation respond, singing or saying on ordinary Lord's Days the portion assigned below (*Alternative* at discretion):

But, on all *Special Days,* Special Responses, found in the "Offices for the Christian Year", take place of those here given.—

Introductory Responses.

LORD'S DAY FIRST IN THE MONTH.— [Is. vi. 3.]

Holy, Holy, Holy, is the Lord of hosts !
The whole earth is full of His glory.

Alternative. [Ps. xciii. 5.]

Thy testimonies are very sure :
Holiness becometh Thine House, O Lord ! for ever.

LORD'S DAY SECOND IN THE MONTH.— [Ps. xli. 13.]

Blessed be the Lord God of Israel from everlasting, and to everlasting!—
Amen! and Amen!

Alternative. [Is. xl. 9.]

O Zion, that bringest good tidings —
Get thee up into the high mountain!
O Jerusalem, that bringeth good tidings —
Lift up thy voice with strength!
Lift it up!

LORD'S DAY THIRD IN THE MONTH.— [Ps. xcix. 1.]

The Lord reigneth :—
Let the people tremble!
He sitteth between the Cherubims :—
Let the earth be moved!

Alternative. [Ps. lxxvii. 13.]

Thy way, O God! is in the Sanctuary :—
Who is so great a God, as our God?

LORD'S DAY FOURTH IN THE MONTH.— [Ps. xxvi. 8.]

Lord! I have loved the habitation of Thy House,
And the place where Thine honor dwelleth.

Alternative. [Ps. cxxxii. 8, 9.]

Arise! O Lord! into Thy rest!—
Thou and the Ark of Thy strength!
Let Thy priests be clothed with righteousness :
And let Thy saints shout for joy.

LORD'S DAY FIFTH IN THE MONTH.— [Is. xxvi. 4.]

Trust ye in the Lord, for ever!
For in the Lord Jehovah is everlasting strength.

III. REHEARSING OF THE LAW.— [All still stand]

Minister reads any one, or more, of these three portions, viz., Decalogue [Ex. xx, 1, 3-17]; The Lord's Summary [Mat. xxii, 37-40]; Beatitudes [Mat. v, 3-10] : but always Decalogue and The Lord's Summary on all Special Lord's Days. Afterwards, may be sung or said, I K. viii, 57, 58, as a Response ; though this perhaps is seldom needed.—

IV. GENERAL CONFESSION.— [In the INVITATION, all still stand ; in PRAYER, all kneel.]

Minister first utters as Invitation, any one, or more, of the following portions, with the last one : — Ps. xxxiv, 18 : Prov. xxviii, 13 ; I Jn. i, 8 ; I Jn. i, 9 ; Is. lv, 7 ; I Jn. ii, 1 (last part) : Mat. xi, 28 ; Mat. v, 6 ; Heb. iv, 16.

Minister then, while all kneel, utters the Prayers following, (found in the completed book), or any others of like import. If these forms are used, all join audibly in the Suffrages [printed in small capitals].

These Prayers, which are very brief, consist of—1. Confession of Sin :—2. Petition for Pardon ; —3. Dedication.

V. PROFESSION OF FAITH.— [All stand.]

[When persons are introduced into the membership of the Church, V. Profession of Faith, and VI. Declaration of Grace, are incorporated into the special " Service of Introduction to Membership", which then takes the place of V and VI as here given.—The same rule applies when any persons in infancy, or under guardianship, are baptized : The " Service of Baptism" then takes the place of V and VI as here given.]—

All standing unite with audible voice to profess their faith.—Minister, at discretion, recites as Invitation, Rom. x, 10 —

Apostles' Creed.

I BELIEVE in God — The Father Almighty,
Maker of Heaven and Earth: —

AND in Jesus Christ — His Only Son, our Lord :
Who was conceived by the Holy Ghost ;
Born of the Virgin Mary :
Suffered under Pontius Pilate ;
Was crucified, dead, and buried :
He descended into Hell [Hades] :
The Third Day He rose from the dead :
He ascended into Heaven :
And sitteth at the Right Hand of God the Father Almighty :
From thence He shall come
To judge the Quick and the Dead.

I BELIEVE in the Holy Ghost :
The Holy Catholic Church :
The Communion of Saints :
The Forgiveness of Sins :
The Resurrection of the Body :
And the Life Everlasting.—

AMEN !

VI. DECLARATION OF GRACE.— [All still stand.]

Minister addresses Congregation, using two or more of the following portions of
Holy Scripture, beside the *Benediction.*—

[This is omitted at discretion : except that it is used on all Special Lord's Days.]

Comforting Words of Grace.—

Jn. iii, 16 : Rom. v. 21 :	Rom. v, 1, 2 :
Rom. viii, 1 :	Is. xliv, 22 : Gal. iv, 7 :
Eph. ii, 19 :	Rom. viii. 28 :
II Cor. xiii. 14.	

VII. THE GREAT DOXOLOGY.—

All still standing unite without announcement in singing or saying—

Gloria In Excelsis.

1 **G**LORY BE TO | GOD ON | HIGH!
AND ON EARTH. | PEACE! GOOD | WILL TOWARDS | MEN!

2 WE PRAISE THEE; WE BLESS THEE; WE | WORSHIP | THEE:
WE GLORIFY THEE; WE GIVE THANKS TO | THEE; FOR | THY GREAT | GLORY—
3 O LORD GOD, | HEAVENLY | KING!—
GOD THE | FATHER | AL- | MIGHTY!

4 O LORD! THE ONLY-BEGOTTEN SON, | JESUS | CHRIST!
O LORD GOD! LAMB OF | GOD! | SON * OF THE | FATHER!
5 THAT TAKEST AWAY THE | SINS * OF THE | WORLD!—
HAVE MERCY | UPON | US!
6 THOU THAT TAKEST AWAY THE | SINS * OF THE | WORLD!—
HAVE MERCY | UPON | US!
7 THOU THAT TAKEST AWAY THE | SINS * OF THE | WORLD!—
RE- | CEIVE OUR | PRAYER!
8 THOU THAT SITTEST AT THE RIGHT HAND OF | GOD THE | FATHER!—
HAVE MERCY | UPON | US!

9 FOR THOU | ONLY * ART | HOLY;
THOU | ONLY | ART THE | LORD.

10 THOU ONLY, O CHRIST! WITH THE | HOLY | GHOST,
ART MOST HIGH IN THE | GLORY * OF | GOD THE | FATHER.—

A- | MEN!

_____

VIII. GENERAL PRAYER.—

While all kneel, Minister utters first the short *Prayer for the Day*, (found in "*Offices for the Christian Year*"). At the end of this, and of all other Prayers, all say "AMEN!"—Minister then utters an extemporaneous *Prayer;* or at his discretion, uses *The Litany* (in whose Suffrages all join audibly), or any other proper and edifying forms. In the complete Service-book, such forms are provided—mostly those that have for centuries been used in Christian Worship. Afterwards, he utters *An Ancient Prayer of the Eastern Church*, commonly called "*A Prayer of St. Chrysostom*"; at the end of which, he thus declares—

And now—O Thou that seest the heart!—
We lift up our hearts in silence unto Thee!—

Here, Minister pauses in his utterance for about the time of one minute, while each Worshipper silently addresses God—

SILENT PRAYER.

The silence is broken by the voices of all joining in

The Lord's Prayer. [Mat. vi. 9—13]

OUR FATHER—WHICH ART IN HEAVEN!—
HALLOWED BE THY NAME!
THY KINGDOM COME!
THY WILL BE DONE IN EARTH AS IT IS IN HEAVEN!
GIVE US, THIS DAY, OUR DAILY BREAD.
AND FORGIVE US OUR DEBTS, AS WE FORGIVE OUR DEBTORS.
AND LEAD US NOT INTO TEMPTATION;
BUT DELIVER US FROM EVIL.
FOR THINE IS THE KINGDOM, AND THE POWER, AND THE GLORY, FOR
EVER.

AMEN!

IX. MATIN PSALTER FOR THE DAY.— [All stand.]

Minister announces the Day by its Calendar Number and Name, e.g. "*Twentieth Calendar Day—Lord's Day Ninth after Nativity, Matin Psalter.*"—

The portion of the Psalter appointed for that Day and Morning is then sung or read, *always responsively*. When sung, it is in the simplest and plainest chant.

[This Outline of the Service does not contain the Psalter.]

25

X. MATIN HYMN FOR THE DAY.—

All immediately join without announcement, in singing the Metrical Hymn of
Praise for that Day and Morning, using either of the two selections given
below for each day. On all Special Days, Special Hymns (found in " *Offices
for the Christian Year*") take place of these. Minister, at discretion, announces any other metrical hymn of praise instead of those here given. If
no such announcement is made, one of those given below is used. This
singing always ends with the *Christian Doxology* in the same metre. The
numbers given below, refer to the Hymn Book entitled " Songs of the
Church".

[This singing is in a tune simple or familiar, in which all join with vigor as an act of direct
praise to God. Each Hymn is supplied with its own particular tune. Prelude, if played,
which is not requisite, consists merely of the first strain of the tune to be sung. Interludes
are entirely omitted. It is preferable that Organ and Choir supply the harmony, while
Congregation sing in unison].—

Metrical Hymns of Praise.

LORD'S DAY FIRST IN THE MONTH.—

Hymn 42 [L.M]—Before Jehovah's awful Throne—.
or, Hymn 9 [c.m.—omit 2d stanza]—This is the day the Lord hath made—.

LORD'S DAY SECOND IN THE MONTH.—

Hymn 136 [c.m.]—O God! We praise Thee, and confess—.
or, Hymn 40 [L.M.—omit 4th stanza]—High in the heavens, Eternal God!—

LORD'S DAY THIRD IN THE MONTH.—

Hymn 116 [L.M.—no Dox. added]—O Holy, Holy, Holy Lord!—
or, Hymn 69 [s.m.]—Lord! In this sacred hour—.

LORD'S DAY FOURTH IN THE MONTH.—

Hymn 893 [6s & 7s]—Lord! Thy glory fills the heaven—.
or, Hymn 48 [L.M.]—With glory clad, with strength arrayed—.

LORD'S DAY FIFTH IN THE MONTH.—

Hymn 78 [s s]—Blest be Thou, O God of Israel!—

XI. OFFERTORY.—

After the Hymn, while the benevolent offerings of the Congregation are being collected by the proper officers, Minister utters any of the following sentences of Holy Scripture. Each sentence is succeeded at discretion by a brief Response on Organ.

The Offertory is used at the same service with the Lord's Supper, and at any other services to which the Rules of the Church may specially assign it.—

Acts xx, 35 "Remember.&c.":	II Cor. viii, 9 :	Mat. vi. 19, 20, 21 :	Mat. vii, 12 :
II Cor. ix, 6 :	Heb. vi, 10 :	II Cor. ix. 7. 8:	I Tim.vi, 17, 18,19:
Heb. xiii, 16 :	I Ju. iii, 17 :	Ps. xli, 1 :	Prov. xix. 17 :
Prov. iii, 9 :	I Cor. xvi, 2 (omit last clause):	Mat. x, 8 "Freely."&c.:	Ecc. xi, 1 :
Prov. xiii, 7 :	Is. xxxii, 8 :	Prov. xi, 25 :	Lk. vi, 36 :
Lk. vi, 38 :	Prov. xxi. 13 :	Deut. xv, 11 :	Mat. v. 7.

XII. NOTICES.—

[Such only as are needful and appropriate to the Day and the House of God.]

XIII. SCRIPTURE LESSONS FOR THE DAY.—

Portions of Holy Scripture as appointed in the Table of Scripture Lessons (1st, from Old Testament; 2d, from Gospels), read by Minister.—

XIV. MATIN CHANT FOR THE DAY.—

All standing, immediately join in singing or saying, the Morning Chant for the Day.

On all *Special Days*, Special Chants (found in the " *Offices for the Christian Year*".) take place of those here given.—

[This Chanting, which may be Antiphonal or otherwise,—is simple, and may be unisonous ; that by it, *All* may directly praise God.]

Chants.

LORD'S DAY FIRST IN THE MONTH.— (Ps. cxlv. 1, 3–5, 10, 13, 17, 18, 21.)

1 I WILL extol Thee, my | God ! O | King !—
   And I will bless Thy | Name for | ever * and | ever.
2 Great is the Lord, and greatly | to be | praised :
   And His | greatness * is | un-searchable.
3 One generation shall praise Thy | works * to an- | other,
   And shall de-clare Thy | mighty | acts.
4 I will speak of the glorious honor | of Thy | Majesty,
   And | of Thy | wondrous | works.
5 All Thy works shall | praise Thee, * O | Lord !—
   And Thy | Saints shall | bless | Thee.
6 Thy Kingdom is an ever- | lasting | Kingdom,
   And Thy Dominion endureth | throughout * all | gener-ations.

7 THE Lord is righteous in | all His | ways,
   And holy in | all | His | works.
8 The Lord is nigh unto all them that | call up-on | Him,
   To all that | call up-on | Him in | truth.
9 My mouth shall speak the | praise * of the | Lord :
   And let all Flesh bless His Holy | Name, for | ever * and |
   ever !—

10 GLORY Be to the Father ! and | to the | Son !
   And | to the | Holy | Ghost !—
11 As it was in the Beginning, is Now, and | Ever | shall be,—
   World with- | out end. | —A- | MEN !

LORD'S DAY SECOND IN THE MONTH.— (Ps. civ. 1–5, 24, 33–35.)

1 BLESS the Lord, | O my | Soul !
   O Lord ! my | God ! * Thou art | very | great :
2 Thou art clothed with | honor * and | majesty :
   Who coverest Thyself with | light as | with a | garment ;
3 Who stretchest out the Heavens | like a | curtain ;
   Who layeth the beams of His | chambers | in the | waters ;

⁴ Who maketh the | clouds His | chariot ;
  Who walketh up- | on the | wings * of the | wind :
⁵ Who maketh His | angels | spirits ;
  His | ministers *, a | flaming | fire ;
⁶ Who laid the foundations | of the | Earth,
  That it should not be re- | moved | for | ever.
⁷ O LORD ! how manifold | are Thy | works !
  In wisdom hast Thou made them all : The | Earth is | full * of
  Thy | riches.

⁸ I WILL sing unto the Lord as | long * as I | live :
  I will sing praise to my | God * while I | have my | being.
⁹ My meditation of Him | shall be | sweet :
  I will be glad in the Lord. | BLESS thou * the | Lord,* O
  my | soul !

¹⁰ GLORY Be to the Father ! and | to the | Son !
  And | to the | Holy | Ghost !—
¹¹ As it was in the Beginning, is Now, and | Ever | shall be,—
  World with- | out end. | —A- | MEN !

LORD'S DAY THIRD IN THE MONTH.—   [Ps. lxviii. 1, 7. 8. 11. 18. 19. 32. 35.]

¹ LET God arise ! Let His | enemies * be | scattered !
    Let them also that | hate Him | flee be-fore | Him !

² O GOD ! When Thou wentest forth be- | fore Thy | People,
  When Thou didst march through the | wilder-ness : the | Earth
  | shook :
³ The Heavens also dropped at the | presence * of | God :
  Even Sinai itself was moved at the presence of God, the | God
  | of | Israel.
⁴ The Lord | gave the | Word :
  Great was the company of | those that | published | it.

⁵ THOU hast as- | cended * on | high,
  Thou hast led cap- | tivi- | ty | captive :
⁶ Blessed be the Lord ! Who daily loadeth | us with | benefits,
  Even the | God of | our Sal- | vation.

⁷ SING unto God, Ye | Kingdoms * of the | Earth !
O sing | praises * un- | to the | Lord !
⁸ O God, Thou art terrible out of Thy | Holy | Places !
The God of Israel is He that giveth | strength and * power un-
| to His | People.
⁹ GLORY Be to the Father ! and | to the | Son !
And | to the | Holy | Ghost !—
¹⁰ As it was in the Beginning, is Now, and | Ever | shall Be,
World with- | out end.— | A- | MEN !

LORD'S DAY FOURTH IN THE MONTH.—   [Ps. lxxxix, 1, 5. 6. 11, 13, 14, 18, 52.]

¹ I WILL sing of the mercies of the | Lord, for | ever :
With my mouth will I make known Thy | faithful-ness to
| all * gener- | ations.

² AND the Heavens shall praise Thy | wonders, * O | Lord :
Thy faithfulness also, in the Congre- | gation | of the | Saints.
³ For, who in the Heaven can be com- | pared * unto the | Lord !
Who among the sons of the mighty can be | likened * un- | to
the | Lord !
⁴ The Heavens | are | Thine,
The Earth | al- | so is | Thine :
⁵ As for the World and the fulness thereof, | Thou hast | founded
them.
Thou | hast a | mighty | Arm :
⁶ Strong | is Thy | Hand.
And | high is | Thy Right | Hand.
⁷ Justice and Judgment are the habitation of | Thy | Throne ;
Mercy and Truth shall | go be- | fore Thy | Face.

⎰ ⁸ THE Lord is | our De- | fence ;
⎱   And the Holy One of | Is-rael | is our | King.

⁹ BLESSED Be the Lord for | Ever- | more —
A- | MEN ! and | A- | MEN !

¹⁰ GLORY Be to the Father ! and | to the | Son !
And | to the | Holy | Ghost !—
¹¹ As it was in the Beginning, is Now, and | Ever | shall be,
World with- | out end. | —A- | MEN !

¹ THE Lord reigneth : Let the | Earth re- | joice !
Let the multitude of | Isles be | glad there- | of !

² CLOUDS and darkness are | round a-bout | Him :
Righteousness and judgment are the | habi-tation | of His |
Throne.
³ A fire | goeth ˙ be- | fore Him,
And burneth up His | ene-mies | round a- | bout.
⁴ His lightnings en- | lightened ˙ the | World :
The | Earth | saw and | trembled.
⁵ The hills melted like wax at the | presence ˙ of the | Lord,
At the presence of the | Lord ˙ of the | whole | Earth.

⁶ THE Heavens de- | clare His | righteousness,
And all the | People | see His | Glory.

⁷ ZION heard | and was | glad ;
And the Daughters of Judah rejoiced be- | cause ˙ of Thy |
judg-ments, O | Lord !
˙ For Thou, Lord ! art high a- | bove ˙ all the | earth :
Thou art ex- | alted ˙ far a- | bove all | gods.

⁹ REJOICE in the | Lord, Ye | righteous !
And give thanks at the re- | membrance ˙ of | His | Holiness !

¹⁰ GLORY Be to the Father ! and | to the | Son !
And | to the | Holy | Ghost !—
¹¹ As it was in the Beginning, is Now, and | Ever | shall be,
World with- | out end. | —A- | MEN !

XV. SERMON.—

[Congregation sit.]

In length, generally not less than fifteen, nor more than thirty, minutes. When
the Lord's Supper is to be a part of the Service, the *Sermon* is made very
short, or omitted altogether.—

XVI. HYMN.—

Generally, in metre; and announced and read by minister.—Sung by choir, or Congregation, all standing. Preludes and Interludes on Organ at discretion.—When the Lord's Supper is to be celebrated. its Special Service takes the place of XV, XVI. XVII, XVIII.—

XVII. CLOSING PRAYER.—

Uttered by Minister.—All kneeling, and joining audibly in the Suffrage " AMEN!" at end of Prayer, and again at end of Benediction.—*The Prayer*, which is always *very brief*, is either extemporaneous, or according to a prepared form.—*The Benediction*, which is in any of the forms found in Holy Scripture, is incorporated with the Prayer which it concludes.—All remain kneeling till the Organ sounds, or for at least a quarter of a minute after the last " AMEN!"—

XVIII. ORGAN VOLUNTARY.—

Beginning about a quarter of a minute after *Benediction.*—Continuing for about five minutes, or till Assembly has generally dispersed.—

Lord's Day.—Evening Service.

ORDER.

I. Organ Voluntary.
II. { Introductory:—
     { Response.
III. First Vesper Psalm (*Psalter*).
IV. The Chant.
V. The Prayer.
VI. Second Vesper Psalm (*Psalter*).
VII. The Metrical Hymn of Worship.
VIII. Offertory (*when appointed*).
IX. Notices (*when needful*).
X. The Lessons of Holy Scripture.
XI. Hymn.
XII. Sermon.
XIII. Metrical Hymn.
XIV. { Prayer:—
      { Benediction.
XV. Organ Voluntary.

If the Evening Service includes *Baptism, Introduction to Membership*, or *The Lord's Supper*, the Order for Morning Service is followed instead of that for the Evening.

Or, retaining the Evening Order, *Baptism* and *Introduction to Membership* take the place of III; and *The Lord's Supper* takes the place of XII, XIII, XIV, XV :—XII is however, if desirable, retained in a much shortened form.

Lord's Day.

EVENING SERVICE.

I. ORGAN VOLUNTARY.—

[Congregation assemble.]

Beginning as Minister enters — not earlier than five minutes before the time appointed for Service :

Ending, three minutes after the time.—

II. INTRODUCTION.—

[All stand.]

1.—Minister pronounces one or more of the portions of Holy Scripture set forth as *Introductories ;* or the portion set forth below, which the Choir are about to sing.—

2.—Choir or Congregation respond, singing or saying on ordinary Lord's Days the portion assigned below (*Alternative* at discretion):

But, on all *Special Days,* Special Responses, found in the "Offices for the Christian Year", take place of those here given.—

Introductory Responses.

LORD'S DAY FIRST IN THE MONTH.—

[Zech. xiv, 7, 8.]

It shall come to pass
That at Evening-time it shall be light.
And it shall be in that day
That living waters shall go out from Jerusalem.

Alternative.

[Is. lxii. 6.]

I have set Watchmen upon thy walls, O Jerusalem !
Which shall never hold their peace, day nor night :
Ye that make mention of the Lord !—
Keep not silence !

LORD'S DAY SECOND IN THE MONTH.— [Ps. lxxx. 1.]

> Give ear, O Shepherd of Israel!
> Thou That leadest Joseph like a flock—
> Thou That dwellest between the Cherubims—
> Shine forth!

Alternative. [Ps. xxxiii. 22.]

> Let Thy mercy, O Lord! be upon Us!
> According as We hope in Thee.

LORD'S DAY THIRD IN THE MONTH.— [Ps. xxix. 11.]

> The Lord will give strength unto His People :
> The Lord will bless His People with Peace.

Alternative. [Ps. cxiii. 3.]

> From the Rising of the Sun
> Unto the Going down of the same.
> The Lord's Name is to be praised.

LORD'S DAY FOURTH IN THE MONTH.— [Ps. xlii. 1.]

> As the hart panteth after the water-brooks,
> So panteth my Soul after Thee, O God!

Alternative. [Rev. xv, 3.]

> Great and marvellous are Thy works,
> Lord God Almighty!
> Just and true are Thy ways,
> Thou King of Saints!

LORD'S DAY FIFTH IN THE MONTH.— [Ps. lxxxix. 15.]

> Blessed is the People that know the joyful sound!
> They shall walk, O Lord! in the light of Thy countenance.

35

III. FIRST VESPER PSALM.—

Minister announces the Day by its Calendar Number and Name, e.g. "*Forty-first Calendar Day, Lord's Day Next After Ascension; First Vesper Psalm*"; etc. The portion of the Psalter appointed for that Day and Evening is then sung or read, *always responsively.* When sung, it is in the simplest and plainest chant.—

[This Outline of the Service does not contain the Psalter.]

IV. CHANT FOR THE DAY.— [All still stand.]

All immediately join in singing or saying the Evening Chant for the Day.

On all *Special Days*, Special Chants (found in the "*Offices for the Christian Year*"), take place of those here given.—

[This Chanting, which may be Antiphonal or otherwise, is simple, and may be unisonous ; that by it, *All* may directly praise God.]

Chants.

LORD'S DAY FIRST IN THE MONTH.— [Ps. lx, 1, 2, 7–11, 13, 14.]

¹ I WILL praise Thee, O Lord ! with my | whole | heart ;
    I will show forth | all Thy | mar-vellous | works.
² I will be glad and re- | joice in | Thee :
    I will sing praise to Thy | Name, O | Thou Most | High !

³ THE Lord shall en- | dure for | ever :
    He hath pre- | pared His | Throne for | judgment.
⁴ And He shall judge the | World in | righteousness,
    He shall minister judgment to the | People | in | uprightness.
⁵ The Lord also will be | a refuge * for the op- | pressed,
    A | refuge * in | times of | trouble.
⁶ And they that know Thy Name, will put their | trust in | Thee ;
    For Thou, Lord ! hast not forsaken | them that | seek | Thee.

⁷ SING praises to the Lord which | dwelleth * in | Zion :
    Declare among the | People | His | doings.

⁸ Have mercy upon | me, O | Lord !
   Thou that liftest me | up · from the | Gates of | Death !
⁹ That I may show forth all Thy Praise in the Gates of the | Daughter · of | Zion
   I will re- | joice in | Thy Sal- | vation.—

¹⁰ GLORY Be to the Father ! and | to the | Son !
   And | to the | Holy | Ghost !—
¹¹ As it was in the Beginning, is Now, and | Ever | shall Be,
   World with- | out end.— | A- | MEN !

LORD'S DAY SECOND IN THE MONTH.— [Ps. lxv, 1, 2 : lxxxvi. 5. 6. 9. 10 12]

¹ PRAISE waiteth for Thee, O | God ! in | Zion :
   And unto | Thee · shall the | Vow · be per- | formed.
² O Thou that | hearest | prayer !
   Unto | Thee shall | all flesh | come.

³ FOR Thou, Lord ! art good, and | ready · to for- | give ;
   And plenteous in mercy unto | all · them that | call · upon | Thee.
⁴ Give ear, O Lord ! un- | to my | prayer ;
   And attend to the | voice · of my | suppli- | cations.

⁵ ALL Nations whom thou hast made shall come and worship before | Thee, O | Lord !
   And shall | glori- | fy Thy | Name.
⁶ For Thou art great and doest | wondrous | things :
   Thou | art | God a- | lone.
⁷ I will praise Thee, O Lord, my God ! with | all my | heart :
   And I will glorify Thy | Name for | ever- | more.

⁸ GLORY Be to the Father ! and | to the | Son !
   And | to the | Holy | Ghost !—
⁹ As it was in the Beginning, is Now, and | Ever | shall be,
   World with- | out end. | —A- | MEN !

LORD'S DAY THIRD IN THE MONTH.— [Ps. xciii.]

¹ THE Lord reigneth ; He is | clothed with | majesty ;
   The Lord is clothed with strength wherewith | He hath | girded · Him- | self :

37

² The World also | is es- | tablished,
That | it can- | not be | moved.
³ Thy Throne is es- | tablished ˙ of | old .
Thou | art from | Ever- | lasting.
⁴ The floods have lifted | up, O | Lord !
The floods have lifted up their voice ; the | floods lift | up their
| waves.
⁵ The Lord on high is mightier than the noise of | many | waters,
Yea than the | mighty | waves ˙ of the | sea.
⁶ Thy Testimonies are | very | sure :
Holiness becometh Thine | House, O | Lord ! for | ever.—

⁷ GLORY Be to the Father ! and | to the | Son !
And | to the | Holy | Ghost !—
⁸ As it was in the Beginning, is Now, and | Ever | shall be,
World with- | out end.— | A- | MEN !

LORD'S DAY FOURTH IN THE MONTH.— [Ps. viii.]

¹ O LORD, our Lord ! how excellent is Thy Name in | all the |
Earth !
Who hast set Thy | glory ˙ a- | bove the | Heavens.
² Out of the mouth of | babes and | sucklings
Hast | Thou or- | dain-ed | strength
³ Because | of Thine | enemies,
That Thou mightest still the | ene-my | and ˙ the a- | venger.

⁴ WHEN I consider Thy Heavens, the | work ˙ of Thy | Fingers,
The Moon and the | Stars, which | Thou ˙ hast or- | dained ;
⁵ What is man, that Thou art | mindful ˙ of | him ?
And the son of | man, that | Thou ˙ visitest | him ?
⁶ For Thou hast made him a little | lower ˙ than the | Angels,
And hast crowned | him with | glo-ry and | honor.
⁷ Thou madest him to have dominion over the | works ˙ of Thy |
Hands :
Thou hast put all | things | under ˙ his | feet—
⁸ All sheep and oxen, yea, and the | beasts ˙ of the | field ;
The fowl of the air, and the fish of the sea, and whatsoever |
passeth ˙ through the | paths ˙ of the | seas.

⁹ O | LORD, our | Lord !
How excellent is Thy | Name in | all the | Earth !—

38

10 GLORY Be to the Father! and | to the | Son!
And | to the | Holy | Ghost!—
11 As it was in the Beginning, is Now, and | Ever | shall be,
World with- | out end. | —A- | MEN!

LORD'S DAY FIFTH IN THE MONTH.— [Ps. lxvii.]

Also for 1) Lord's Day First in Advent ;   14) Mid-Winter Lord's Day .
          8) New Year Eve ;   47) Mid-Year Day ;
         13) Mid-Winter Day ,   48) Mid-Year Lord's Day.

1 **G**OD be merciful unto | Us! and | bless Us!
  And cause His | Face to | shine * upon | Us!
2 That Thy Way may be | known up-on | Earth—
  Thy saving | Health a- | mong all | Nations!
3 Let the People | praise * Thee, O | God!
  Let | all the | People | praise Thee!
4 Oh, let the | Nations * be | glad
  And | sing | for | joy!
5 For Thou shalt judge the | People | righteously.
  And govern the | Nations | upon | Earth.
6 Let the People | praise Thee, * O | God!
  Let all the | People | praise | Thee!
7 Then shall the | Earth * yield her | increase :
  And God, | even * our | own * God, shall | bless us.
8 God | shall | bless us,
  And all the ends of the | Earth shall | fear | Him.—

9 GLORY Be to the Father! and | to the | Son!
  And | to the | Holy | Ghost!—
10 As it was in the Beginning, is Now, and | Ever | shall be,
  World with- | out end. | —A- | MEN!

V. GENERAL PRAYER.— [All kneel.]

While all kneel, Minister utters first the short *Prayer for the Day* (found in
"*Offices for the Christian Year*"). At the end of this, and of all other Prayers,
all say "AMEN!"— Minister then utters an extemporaneous *Prayer;* unless
this be the first Service of the Day, in which case, such forms are used as
are provided in the Morning Service. Afterwards, he thus declares—

And now—O Thou that seest the heart!
We lift up our hearts in silence unto Thee!—

Here Minister pauses in his utterance for about the time of one minute, while
each worshipper silently addresses God—

Silent Prayer.

The Silence is broken by the voices of all joining in

The Lord's Prayer. [Mat. vi. 9-13.]

OUR Father—Which art in Heaven!—
Hallowed be Thy Name!
Thy Kingdom come!
Thy will be done in Earth as it is in Heaven!
Give us this day our daily bread.
And forgive us our debts, as we forgive our debtors.
And lead us not into temptation;
But deliver us from evil.
For Thine is the Kingdom, and the Power, and the Glory, for
ever,

AMEN!

SECOND VESPER PSALM. [All stand.]

Minister announces the Day by its Calendar Number and Name, e.g. "*Forty-first
Calendar Day, Lord's Day Next After Ascension; Second Vesper Psalm*".—

The second portion of the Psalter appointed for that Evening is then sung or
read, *always responsively*. When sung, it is in the simplest and plainest
Chant.

[This Outline of the Service does not contain the Psalter.]

VII. VESPER HYMN FOR THE DAY.— <small>[All still stand.]</small>

All immediately join without announcement, in singing the Metrical Hymn of Praise for that Day and Evening, using either of the two selections given below for each day. On all Special Days, Special Hymns (found in " *Offices for the Christian Year*") take place of these. Minister, at discretion, announces any other metrical hymn of praise instead of those here given. If no such announcement is made, one of those given below is used. This singing always ends with the *Christian Doxology* in the same metre. The *numbers* given below, refer to the Hymn Book entitled " Songs of the Church".

<small>[This singing is in a tune simple or familiar, in which all join with vigor as an act of direct praise to God. Each Hymn is supplied with its own particular tune. Prelude, if played, which is not requisite, consists merely of the first strain of the tune to be sung. Interludes are entirely omitted. It is preferable that Organ and Choir supply the harmony, while Congregation sing in unison].—</small>

LORD'S DAY FIRST IN THE MONTH.—

Hymn 41 [L.M.]—Lord God of Hosts, by all adored !—

or, Hymn 68 [s.M.]—Thy Name, Almighty Lord !—

LORD'S DAY SECOND IN THE MONTH.—

Hymn 34 [s.M.]—O Thou above all praise !—

or, Hymn 141 [c.M.—omit 3d stanza]—Great God ! how infinite art Thou !—

LORD'S DAY THIRD IN THE MONTH.—

Hymn 128 [L.M.]—Lord of all being ! Throned afar—.

or, Hymn 887 [L.M.—omit 4th stanza]—My God ! My King ! Thy various praise—.

LORD'S DAY FOURTH IN THE MONTH.—

Hymn 909 [s.P.M.]—The Lord Jehovah reigns—.

or, Hymn 878 [8s & 7s—omit last stanza—no Dox. added]—Praise to Thee,Thou great Creator !—

LORD'S DAY FIFTH IN THE MONTH.—

Hymn 75 [10s & 11s]—O, worship the King, all glorious above !—

VIII.—OFFERTORY.—*As in Morning Service.* [All still stand.]

IX. NOTICES.—*As in Morning Service.* [Congregation sit.]

X. SCRIPTURE LESSONS FOR THE DAY.— [Congregation sit.]

Portions of Holy Scripture as appointed in the Table of Scripture Lessons (1st, from Old Testament: 2d, from the Acts, Epistles, or, Revelation), read by Minister.—

XI. HYMN.— [All stand.]

Generally, in metre; but occasionally a Chant or Anthem is used if desirable.— Generally, announced and read by minister.—Sung by choir, or Congregation, all standing. Preludes and Interludes on Organ, at discretion.

XII. SERMON.—*As in Morning Service.* [Congregation sit.]

XIII. HYMN.—*As in Morning Service.* [All Stand.]

XIV. { CLOSING PRAYER: } *As in Morning Service.*
{ BENEDICTION.— } [All kneel.]

XV. ORGAN VOLUNTARY.—*As in Morning Service.*

42

[These Services, in the Morning, take place of V and VI, and in the Evening, of III.]

Introduction to Membership from Another Church.

I. ANNOUNCEMENT.—Candidates rise and stand.
II. COVENANT BY THE CANDIDATES.—Including the CREED OF THE CHURCH, if no other Candidates are to be received. [See the next Service.]
III. COVENANT BY THE CHURCH.—Church rise and stand.
IV. { DECLARATION OF GRACE, AND } All stand.
    { BENEDICTION.— }
V. ASCRIPTION.—All stand.

Introduction to Membership, By Confirmation, or By Baptism.

I. ANNOUNCEMENT.—Candidates present themselves before Pulpit.

II. CONFESSION OF FAITH —

Preface to Church Creed.

[Usually omitted : but should be publicly read at least once in each year. It is fitting that it be read on the Pentecost Day, if any Candidates be then present.]

THIS Church expresses its views of Christian Doctrine in an extended CREED, the same in substance with that of other Churches in its Denominational Connection :—a Creed, in general accordance with which it requires that the public teachings of this Sanctuary shall be conducted ; and which, as embodying in convenient form the great Truths of Holy Scripture, is commended to your careful study, your intelligent acceptance, and your devout contemplation

But, this Church, viewing Itself as first and essentially *Christian*, and only subordinately *Denominational ;*—rejoicing therefore to express Its fellowship with Christ's whole visible Church of every Name, thus avoiding even the semblance of the sin of Schism, which, for the sake of things not essential in the Gospel, divides the Church of Christ which is His Body ;—and, not assuming to exclude from its fellowship any whom the Master has plainly accepted, but rather seeking to follow the precept of the Apostle Paul, to receive him that is weak in the Faith but not to doubtful disputations ;—this Church requires as a test of *Admission to Its Fellowship,* a Profession of Faith in only those plain facts of the Gospel in which all throughout the World, who follow Christ, can unite.

THIS, then, is the Ancient and Universal Faith of the Christian Church, which, in company with Us, You now profess.—   [Or, the Apostles' Creed is used.]

[The Church rise, and with the Candidates, join audibly.]

The Church Creed.

I BELIEVE in God — the Father, the Son, and the Holy Ghost:

I BELIEVE in His Creative Power,
His Perfect Providence,
His Infinite Dominion,
And His Everlasting Love.

I CONFESS Jesus Christ, — His Only Son,
God Manifest in the Flesh,
Our Lord and Savior ;
Through Whom Alone is the Forgiveness of Sins :
Who was crucified for Us ;
Who ascended into Heaven :
Who reigneth in the Glory of the Father.

I CONFESS the Holy Ghost, — the Sanctifier,
Through Whose gift alone is wrought the Renewal of the
    heart :
Who leadeth to Repentance ;
Who worketh Love ;
Who giveth the new Life of faith upon the Son of God.

I BELIEVE in the Holy Scriptures — the Word of God.

I CONFESS one Holy and Universal Church of Christ, in Whom
    the Whole Family in Heaven and Earth is named :
I Acknowledge one Baptism after His command ;
And the Communion in His Body and Blood in remembrance of
    Him.

I LOOK for the glorious Coming of the Lord ;
The Resurrection of the Dead :
And the just Recompenses of the World to Come.

AMEN !   [Church resume their seats.]

III.   Covenant by The Candidates.—
IV.   Baptism ; or Recognition of Previous Baptism.—Immediately before the Baptism, Church rise.
V.   Covenant by the Church.—Church still stand.
VI.   Declaration of Grace, and Benediction.—All stand.
VII.   Ascription.—All stand.

The Lord's Supper.

When the Lord's Supper occurs on any Lord's Day, generally in the morning, the Sermon is much shortened. The Communion Service then proceeds as follows.—

I. THE CHIEF SONG.— [All stand.]

Without announcement, All rise, and immediately join in singing or saying—

Te Deum Laudamus.

[If sung as an Anthem, the larger print indicates the Chorus parts, in which all join.]

1 WE Praise | Thee, O | God!
    We acknowledge | Thee to | be the | Lord.

2 All the Earth doth | worship | Thee,
    The | Father | ever- | lasting.

3 To Thee all Angels cry | a- | loud,
    The Heavens, and | all the | powers there- | in.

4 To Thee | Cherubim * and | Seraphim,
    Con- | tinu-al- | ly do | cry.

5 Holy, | Holy, | Holy,
    Lord | God of | Saba- | oth!

6 Heaven and | Earth are | full
    Of the | majes-ty | of thy | Glory!

7 The glorious company of the Apostles | Praise | Thee.

    The goodly fellowship of the | Prophets | Praise Thee.

8 The noble army of Martyrs | Praise | Thee.

    The Holy Church throughout all the world | Doth ac- | know-
                                            ledge | Thee.

9 The Father, of an | infi-nite | majesty:
    Thine adorable, | true and | only | Son:

10 Also the | Holy | Ghost,
    The | Com | fort- | er.

11 Thou art the King of | glory, * O | Christ!

    Thou art the everlasting | Son * of the | Fa- | ther!

12 When Thou tookest upon Thee to de- | liver | Man,
    Thou didst humble Thyself to be | born | of a | virgin.

13 When Thou hadst overcome the | sharpness * of | death,
    Thou didst open the Kingdom of | Heaven to | all be- | lievers.

14 THOU SITTEST AT THE RIGHT HAND OF GOD, IN THE GLORY | OF THE | FATHER.
WE BELIEVE THAT THOU SHALT | COME TO | BE OUR | JUDGE.
15 WE THEREFORE PRAY THEE, | HELP THY | SERVANTS,
WHOM THOU HAST REDEEMED | WITH THY | PRECIOUS | BLOOD.
16 MAKE THEM TO BE NUMBERED | WITH THY | SAINTS,
IN | GLORY | EVER- | LASTING.
17 O LORD, SAVE THY PEOPLE, AND | BLESS THINE | HERITAGE !
GOVERN THEM AND | LIFT THEM | UP FOR | EVER.
18 DAY BY DAY WE | MAGNI-FY | THEE ;
AND WE WORSHIP THY NAME EVER, | WORLD WITH- | OUT | END.
19 VOUCHSAFE, O LORD, TO KEEP US THIS DAY | WITHOUT | SIN ;
O LORD, HAVE MERCY UPON US !   HAVE | MER-CY UP- | ON | US!
20 O LORD, LET THY MERCY BE UP- | ON | US,
AS OUR | TRUST | IS IN | THEE.
21 O LORD, IN THEE | HAVE I | TRUSTED ;
LET ME | NEVER | BE CON- | FOUNDED!   [LET ME | NEVER | BE CON- | FOUNDED !]

II. ANNOUNCEMENT.—

[Congregation sit.]

III. THE WORDS OF THE INSTITUTION.—

[Congregation sit.]

Combined from I Cor. xi, 23-25 ; Mat. xxvi. 26-29 ; Lk. xxii, 20.

IV. INVITATION AND EXHORTATION.—

[Congregation sit.]

After the Invitation, Minister taking his place by the Table, thus addresses Congregation—

LIFT up your hearts !—

Congregation respond—

WE LIFT THEM UP UNTO THE LORD.—

V. THE PRAYER.—

Either in the form provided, or extemporaneous. At its close Minister thus
declares —

THEE, mighty God, Heavenly King, We magnify and praise!
With Patriarchs and Prophets, Apostles and Martyrs;
With Thy holy Church throughout all the World;
With the Heavenly Jerusalem, the joyful assembly of the Just on
High;
With the innumerable Company of Angels, and the Archangels
round about Thy Throne, the Heaven of Heavens and all the
Powers therein;
We worship and adore Thy glorious Name,—joining in the Song of
Cherubim and Seraphim, and with united voice singing and
saying —

[Here, all stand, and join aloud in the Seraphic Hymn.]

HOLY! HOLY! HOLY! LORD GOD OF HOSTS!
HEAVEN AND EARTH ARE FULL OF THY GLORY.
GLORY BE TO THEE, O LORD MOST HIGH!

[From Is. vi, 3.]

VI. THE BREAD.—

[Congregation sit : in the PRAYER,
all kneel.]

1. Minister lifts, or lays his hands on, any or all of The Bread ; saying—

THE Lord Jesus, the same Night in which He was
Betrayed, Took Bread—

2. Minister, still holding The Bread, thus speaks; and then utters the PRAYER OF CONSECRATION, always brief.—

AND Blessed It :
So, Let us Pray.—

3. Minister, standing, breaks The Bread with his hands, saying—

WHEN the Lord Jesus had blessed the Bread,
He Brake It—

4. Minister gives The Bread to the Deacons, who stand till he has thus spoken.
He, having seated himself, partakes The Bread : The Deacons distribute toCongregation.
Any omission is signified by rising.

WHEN the Lord Jesus had broken The Bread, He
Gave it to His Disciples, and Said—
"TAKE, Eat : This is My Body Which is Broken
for You ;
"This Do, in Remembrance of Me."

During the Distribution of The Bread, Minister, sitting, occasionally breaks the stillness by uttering slowly and solemnly at intervals, any appropriate Passages of Holy Scripture. But at least half of the time of Distribution is passed in silence.—

Deacons return The Bread into Minister's hands, who replaces it on the Table, while they seat themselves near. He then, when all are seated, serves The Bread to each Deacon ; repeating as above, any Scripture, at discretion.—

III. THE WINE.—

1. Minister pours The Wine into the various Cups; saying—

AFTER the same manner also, the Lord Jesus took The Cup—

2. Minister, lifting or laying his hands on, any or all of the vessels containing The Wine, thus speaks; and then utters the PRAYER OF CONSECRATION, always brief.—

HAVING taken The Cup, He Gave Thanks: So, Let Us Pray.—

3. Minister, retaining one Cup for himself, gives the others to the Deacons, who stand till he has thus spoken. He, having seated himself, partakes The Wine; He then gives the Cup to the Senior Deacon. The Deacons distribute to Congregation Any omission is signified by rising.

AFTER the Lord Jesus had Given Thanks, He gave The Cup to His Disciples, Saying—
"THIS Cup is My Blood of the New Testament,
"Which is shed for many, for the Remission of Sins;
"This Do Ye, as oft as Ye Drink It, in Remembrance of Me."

During Distribution of The Wine, Minister, sitting, occasionally breaks the stillness by uttering slowly and solemnly at intervals, any appropriate Passages of Holy Scripture. But at least half of the time of Distribution is passed in silence.—

Deacons return The Cups into Minister's hands, who replaces them on the Table, while they seat themselves near. He then, when all are seated, serves The Wine to each Deacon; repeating, as above, any Scripture, at discretion.—

VII. THE THANKSGIVING.—

Minister thus declares—

WHEN the Lord Jesus and His Disciples had sung a Hymn, they went out into the Mount of Olives.
So, Let Us, before going hence, Give Thanks, and sing—

Then immediately all, without preliminary reading of the Hymn, and without prelude or interludes on the Organ, rise and sing, always in the same tune.—

Hymn 638 [7s—omit 3d stanza]—At the Lamb's High Feast, We Sing—.

The Great Doxology ("*Gloria In Excelsis*") is used at discretion, instead of this Hymn, if it have not been previously used in the same Service.—

IX. { CLOSING PRAYER: / BENEDICTION.— } *As in the usual Service.*

X. ORGAN VOLUNTARY.—*As in the usual Service.*

Baptism of Infants.

I. ANNOUNCEMENT.—Congregation sit.

II. BAPTISMAL CHANT.—By Choir. Congregation sit.

Minister descends from Pulpit, to the Font. It is fitting that one or more of the Deacons take station near the Pulpit, to assist as may be needed. Candidates are brought forward. Only so much of the Chant is sung, as gives time for all to take their places.

Chant.

[Mark x. 14.]

1 SUFFER little children, and forbid them not to | come * unto | Me,
For of | such * is the | Kingdom * of | Heaven.

[Is. xliv, 3, 4.]

2 I WILL pour My Spirit up- | on thy | seed,
And My | blessing * up- | on thine | offspring :

3 And they shall spring up as a- | mong the | grass,
As | willows * by the | water- | courses.

[Ex. xxxvi, 25, 26.]

4 THEN will I sprinkle clean | water * up- | on you
And | ye | shall be | clean :

5 A new heart also | will I | give you,
And a new spirit | will I | put with- | in you,

6 And I will take away the stony | heart * out of your | flesh,
And I will | give * you a | heart of | flesh.

[Acts ii, 39.]

7 FOR the promise is | unto | you,
And | to your | child- | ren :

8 And to all that are a- | far | off,
Even as many as the | Lord our | God shall | call.

[Ps. ciii, 17, 18.]

9 THE mercy of the Lord is from everlasting to | ever- | lasting
Upon | them that | fear | Him :

10 And His righteousness to | children's | children
To | such as | keep His | covenant.

[Is. xl, 11.]

11 HE shall feed His flock | like a | shepherd :
He shall gather the lambs with His arm, and | carry * them |
in His | bosom.

III. PRAYER.—All kneel.

IV. ADDRESS TO THE PARENTS OR GUARDIANS.—
Very brief.—Congregation sit.

V. PROFESSION OF FAITH.—All standing, join audibly in the *Creed* with the Parents or Guardians.

VI. COVENANT.—All still stand.

Minister thus addresses the Parents or Guardians—

BELOVED :—You bring *this Child* [these children] here to be Baptized.

Do You now solemnly covenant, by God's help, to instruct *this Child* [these children] in the Gospel of our Lord Jesus Christ ; to bring *him* [her *or* them] up in the nurture and admonition of the Lord ; and earnestly to pray and diligently to strive that *he* [she *or* they] renouncing the Devil and all his works, the vain pomp and glory of the World, with all covetous desires of the Same, and all sinful leadings of the Flesh, may walk obediently in the way of God's commandments all the days of *his* [her *or* their] life ?—

Each Parent or Guardian answers—

I THUS COVENANT.

VII. BAPTISM.—All still stand.

Minister, taking each Child on his arm, or leaving it in the arms of the Parent or Guardian, says—

NAME this Child.— [The Parent pronounces the *full* name, without surname.]

Minister then dipping his right hand into the Water, sprinkles the Child's forehead, uttering with each application of Water the Baptismal Formula preceded by the Child's *full Baptismal* name (without surname). He does not conjoin any other word with the Formula ; nor does he add any other sign, symbol, or ceremony in the administration of the water.—

Baptismal Formula.

[*Full Baptismal Name*] ! I BAPTIZE THEE IN THE NAME OF THE FATHER, AND OF THE SON, AND OF THE HOLY GHOST.—AMEN !

[The AMEN is said or sung by all.]

VIII. DECLARATION OF GRACE: with BENEDICTION.—
All still stand.

Offices for the Christian Year.

These Offices in the Book as completed, will embrace the following:—

Introductory, Introductory Response, Prayer for the Day, Psalter (One Lesson for Morning, Two for Evening), *Metrical Hymn of Praise, Old Testament* (One Lesson for Morning, One for Evening), *Gospel, Epistle, Chant.*

But, of these, are given in this Pamphlet, only those *Introductory Responses. Metrical Hymns, and Chants,* which on all *Special Days* take place of those found in the Regular Morning and Evening Service. The Special Days are those which in the *Calendar* (pp. 12–15) begin at the extreme left. The *numbers* of the Metrical Hymns refer to the Hymn Book entitled "Songs of the Church". Every Hymn ends with the Christian Doxology in same metre.

1 **Lord's Day First in Advent.—**

Introductory Response.   [Is. xl, 3.]

PREPARE Ye the way of the Lord !
Make straight in the desert a highway for our God !

8 **New Year Eve.**   13 **Mid Winter Day.**   14 **Mid Winter Lord's Day.**
47 **Mid Year Day.**   48 **Mid Year Lord's Day.—**

Introd. Resp.   [From Ps. cii. 11, 12.]

OUR days are like a shadow that declineth ;
But Thou, O Lord ! shalt endure for ever.

Special Hymns for *all* the above Days—

Morning Hymn, 914 [L.M., omit 3d and 4th stanzas.]—Eternal God ! Eternal King—.

Evening Hymn [C.M. From Sabbath Hymn Book, by permission.]

1 HOPE of our hearts! O Lord, appear.
   Thou glorious Star of day !
Shine forth, and chase the dreary night,
   With all our tears, away.

2 Strangers on earth, we wait for Thee :
   O. leave the Father's throne !
Come with a shout of victory, Lord,
   And claim us as Thine own !

3 Oh, bid the bright archangel then
  The trump of God prepare,
To call Thy saints, the quick, the dead,
To meet thee in the air!

4 No resting-place we seek on earth,
  No loveliness we see ;
Our eye is on the royal crown
Prepared for us and Thee.

5 To FATHER, Son, and Holy Ghost,
  One God, Whom we adore,
Be Glory, as it was, is now,
And shall be evermore !

The Special Chant for *all* the above days, is the same as for Lord's Day Fifth in the Month, Evening. (p. 38.) " *God be merciful unto Us !* "

---

5 **The Natibity Ebe.** 6 **The Natibity Day.** 7 **Lord's Day Next after Natibity** (except Jan. 1).

Introd. Resp.

[Lk. II, 14.]

GLORY to God in the highest !
And on Earth, Peace !
Good Will toward Men !

Special Hymns for all the above Days—

Morning Hymn 926 [6s & 7s]—Hark ! What mean those holy voices ?—
Evening Hymn, 193 [7s—omit 3d stanza.]—Hark ! the herald Angels sing !—

The Special Chant for *The Nativity Eve*, is the *Hymn of the Virgin Mary* [Lk. i, 68–75]; followed by *Doxology of David* [I Chron. xxix, 10–13].

Hymn of the Virgin Mary.

1 **M**Y Soul doth magnify | the | Lord,
    And my spirit hath re- | joiced in | God my | Savior.
2 For He hath regarded the low estate | of His | handmaiden :
    For, behold, from henceforth, all generations | shall | call Me | blessed.
3 For, He that is Mighty hath done to Me | great | things,
    And | Holy | is His | Name ;
4 And His mercy is on them that | fear | Him,
    From generation | to | gener- | ation.
5 He hath showed strength | with His | arm ;
    He hath scattered the proud in the imagi- | nation | of their | hearts.

6 He hath put down the mighty | from their | seats,
And exalted | them of | low de- | gree.
7 He hath filled the hungry | with good | things,
And the rich He hath | sent | empty * a- | way.
8 He hath holpen His | servant | Israel,
In remembrance | of | His | mercy ;
9 As He spake | to our | Fathers,
To Abraham, and | to his | seed, for | ever.

Doxology of David. [1 Ch. xxix. 10–13.]

10 BLESSED be Thou, Lord God of | Israel * our | Father,
For | ever | and | ever.
11 Thine, O Lord! is the greatness, | and the | power,
And the glory, and the | vic-tory, | and the | ma-jesty :
12 For all that is | in the | Heavens
And | in the | Earth is | Thine ;
13 Thine is the | Kingdom * O | Lord!
And Thou art exalted as | Head a- | bove | all.
14 Both riches and honor | come of | Thee,
And Thou | reignest | over | all :
15 And in Thine hand is | power * and | might :
And in Thine hand it is to make great, and to give | strength | unto | all.
16 Now therefore, our God! We | thank | Thee,
And | praise Thy | glo-rious | Name.

17 GLORY Be to the Father! and | to the | Son !
And | to the | Holy | Ghost !—
18 As it was in the Beginning, is Now, and | Ever | shall be,
World with- | out end.— | A- | MEN !

The Special Chant for The Nativity Day, and Lord's Day Next after Nativity (except Jan. 1), is the Hymn of Zacharias (Lk. i, 68–75, 78, 79); followed by Doxology of David (as above) and Gloria Patri.

Hymn of Zacharias.

1 BLESSED be the Lord | God of | Israel ;
For He hath visited | and re- | deemed His | People,
2 And hath raised up an horn of sal- | vation | for Us,
In the house | of His | Servant | David!
3 As He spake by the mouth of His | holy | Prophets
Which have been | since the | World be- | gan :

⁴ That We should be saved | from our | enemies,
  And from the hand of | all that | hate | Us ;
⁵ To perform the Mercy | promised ⁎ to our | Fathers,
  And to remember His | holy | Covenant ;
⁶ The Oath which He sware to our | Father | Abraham—
  That | He would | grant ⁎ unto | Us,
⁷ That We being delivered out of the | hand ⁎ of our | enemies,
  Might | serve Him | without | fear,
⁸ In holiness and righteousness be- | fore | Him,
  All the | days | of our | life—
⁹ Through the tender mercy | of our | God ;
  Whereby the Day-spring from on | high hath | vis-ited | Us,
¹⁰ To give light to them that sit in darkness, and in the | shadow ⁎ of
  | death—
  To guide our feet in- | to the | way of | peace.—

¹¹⁻¹⁷ *Doxology of David* (p. 52).

¹⁸·¹⁹ *Gloria Patri.*

Closing Hymn for *The Nativity Day* (except it be a Lord's Day) is the *Hymn of Simeon*—
[Lk. ii. 29–32].

L ORD ! Now lettest Thou Thy Servant depart in peace,
  According to Thy Word :
For mine eyes have seen Thy Salvation,
Which Thou hast prepared before the face of all People ;
A Light to lighten the Gentiles,
And the Glory of Thy People Israel.

——————

9 𝔑𝔢𝔴 𝔜𝔢𝔞𝔯 𝔇𝔞𝔶.   10 𝔑𝔢𝔴 𝔜𝔢𝔞𝔯 𝔏𝔬𝔯𝔡'𝔰 𝔇𝔞𝔶.—

Introd. Resp.   [From Ps. cii. 24.]

THY Years, O God !
Are throughout all generations.

Special Morning Hymn, 836 [l. m.]—Great God ! We sing that mighty
                                        hand—.
Special Evening Hymn, 838 [l. m.]—Our Helper, God ! — We bless Thy
                                        Name—.

Special Chant.

[Ps. cii, 12, 25-28 ; ciii. 19-22.]

1 THOU, O Lord! shalt en- | dure for | ever ;
 And Thy remembrance unto | all | gener- | ations.

2 OF old hast thou laid the foundation | of the | Earth :
 And the Heavens are the | work of | Thy | hands.

3 They shall perish, but | Thou ˙ shalt en- | dure :
 Yea, all of them shall wax | old | like a | garment ;

4 As a vesture shalt | Thou | change them,
 And | they | shall be | changed :

5 But | Thou ˙ art the | same,
 And Thy | years shall | have no | end.

5 The children of Thy Servants | shall con- | tinue,
 And their seed shall be es- | tab-lished be- | fore | Thee.

7 THE Lord hath prepared His | Throne ˙ in the | heavens ;
 And His Kingdom | ruleth | over | all.

8 Bless the Lord, Ye, His Angels ! that ex- | cel in | strength,
 That do His commandments hearkening unto the | voice | of
 His | Word.

9 Bless Ye the Lord, all | Ye His | Hosts !
 Ye Ministers of | His, that | do His | pleasure.

10 Bless the Lord all His works in all places of | His do- | minion !
 Bless the | Lord, | O My | Soul !--

11, 12 GLORY be to the Father, etc.

Introd. Resp.

[Rev. v, 12.]

WORTHY is the Lamb that was slain
 To receive power, and riches, and wisdom, and strength, and
 honor, and glory, and blessing !

Special Morning Hymn [L.M., 6 lines—From Sabbath Hymn Book, by permission.]

1 Thou art the everlasting Son,
 O Christ ! and, high upon Thy throne,
 Thou art at the right hand of God,
 And hast redeemed Us by Thy blood ;
 And Heaven and Earth are full of Thee,—
 The glory of Thy Majesty !

2 When all the sharpness of our death
 Was overcome in Thy last breath,
 Then didst Thou open wide Heaven's door
 To all believers evermore :
 O Lamb of God ! and Thou wilt come,
 To be our Judge, and take Us home.

3 In Thee we trust: we pray Thee, Lord,
Remember Thy most precious blood!
In honor may we numbered be
With all the noble company,
Who bow before Thy mercy-seat,
And cast their treasures at Thy feet.

4 HAVE mercy on us through Thy blood,
Receive our prayer, O Lamb of God!
For Thou art holy; Thou alone,
At God's right hand, upon His throne,
In all His glory, art adored,
With Thee, O Holy Ghost, ONE LORD

Special Evening Hymn, [L.M., From Sabbath Hymn Book, by permission.]

1 O CHRIST! our King, Creator, Lord!
Saviour of all who trust Thy word!
To them who seek Thee ever near:
Now to our praises bend Thine ear.

2 In Thy dear Cross a grace is found—
It flows from every streaming wound—
Whose power our inbred sin controls,
Breaks the firm bond, and frees our souls!

3 Thou didst create the stars of night;
Yet Thou hast veiled in flesh Thy light—
Hast deigned a mortal form to wear,—
A mortal's painful lot to bear.

4 When Thou didst hang upon the tree,
The quaking earth acknowledged Thee;
When Thou didst there yield up Thy breath
The world grew dark as shades of death.

5 Now in the Father's glory high,
Great Conqu'ror, never more to die,
Us by Thy mighty power defend,
And reign through ages without end!

6 GLORY to The, O God, Most High!
Father, We praise Thy majesty!
The Son, the Spirit, We adore,
One Godhead, blest for evermore!

Special Chant. [Ps. xxii, 1, 16, 18; vi, 1, 2, 4; xxv, 1, 2; cxxxviii, 7, 8.]

1 MY God! My God! Why hast Thou for- | saken | Me?
Why art Thou so | far from | helping | Me?

2 THE assembly of the wicked | have in-closed | Me:
They pierced my | hands | and my | feet.

3 They part my | gar-ments a- | mong them.
And cast | lots up- | on my | vesture.

4 O LORD! rebuke Me | not · in Thine | anger,
Neither chasten | Me · in Thy | hot dis- | pleasure.

5 Have mercy upon Me, O | Lord! for · I am | weak:
O Lord! heal Me; | for My | bones are | vexed.

6 Return, O Lord! de- | liver · My | soul:
O save Me | for Thy | mercies' | sake!

7 UNTO Thee, O Lord! do I lift | up My | soul
O My | God! I | trust in | Thee.

THOUGH I walk in the | midst of | trouble,
Thou | wilt re- | vive | Me:

9 Thou shalt stretch forth Thine hand against the | wrath · of mine | enemies,
And | Thy right | hand shall | save Me.

¹⁰ The Lord will perfect that which con- | cerneth | Me :
Thy mercy, O Lord ! endureth for ever.   Forsake not the | work
of | Thine own | hands. —

^{11, 12} GLORY be to the Father, etc,

---

28 **Cibil Fast Day.**—Any extraordinary Penitential Service. —

Introd. Resp.   [Ps. li. 17.]

THE Sacrifices of God are a broken spirit:
A broken and a contrite heart, O God ! Thou wilt not despise.

Special Hymn, 856 [88 & 74]—Dread Jehovah ! God of Nations !—

Special Chant.   [Ps. cxxx.]

¹ OUT | of the | depths
Have I cried unto | Thee, | O | Lord !
² Lord ! | Hear my | voice !
Let Thine ears be attentive to the | voice * of my | suppli- | cation.
³ If Thou, Lord ! shouldest | mark in- | iquities,
O Lord ! | who | shall | stand ?
⁴ But there is for- | giveness * with | Thee,
That | Thou | mayest * be | feared.
⁵ I wait for the Lord, my | soul doth | wait,
And in His | Word | do I | hope.
⁶ My soul waiteth for the Lord more than they that | watch | for the
| morning :
I say, more than they that | watch | for the | morning.
⁷ Let Israel | hope * in the | Lord :
For with the | Lord | there is | mercy,
⁸ And with Him is | plenteous * re- | demption,
And He shall redeem Israel from | all | his in- | iquities.

^{9, 10} GLORY be to the Father, etc.

Introd. Resp.   [Rev. v, 13, 14.]

BLESSING, and honor, and glory, and power,
Be unto Him that sitteth upon the Throne, and unto the Lamb,
For ever and ever!—AMEN!

Special Morning Hymn, 942 [L.M.]—The morning kindles all the sky—.
Special Evening Hymn, 192 [7s]—Christ, the Lord is risen to-day!—

Special Chant.   [Ps. cxviii, 1, 14-16, 18, 19, 21-24. 26, 28, 29.]

1 OH! give thanks unto the Lord ; for | He is | good :
      Because His | mercy en- | dureth * for | ever.

2 THE Lord is My | strength and | song,
      And is be- | come | My sal- | vation.

3 The voice of rejoicing and salvation is in the tabernacles | of the
      | righteous :
      The right hand of the | Lord | docth | valiantly.

4 The right hand of the | Lord * is ex- | alted :
      The right hand of the | Lord | docth | valiantly.

5 THE Lord hath | chastened * Me | sore :
      But He hath not given Me | over | unto | death.

6 Open to Me the | gates of | righteousness,
      I will go into them, and | I will | praise the | Lord.

7 I will praise Thee ; for | Thou hast | heard Me,
      And art be- | come | My sal- | vation.

8 The stone which the | buil-* ders re- | fused
      Is become the | head stone | of the | corner.

9 This is the | Lord's | doing;
      It is | mar-vellous | in our | eyes.

10 This is the day which the | Lord hath | made ;
      We will re- | joice * and be | glad in | it.

11 Blessed be He That cometh in the | name * of the | Lord ·
      We have | blessed you * out of the | house * of the | Lord.

{ 12 Thou art my God, and | I will | praise Thee :
        Thou art my God, I | will ex- | alt | Thee.

  13 Oh! Give thanks unto the Lord ; for | He is | good :
        For His | mercy * en- | dureth * for | ever.—

14, 15 GLORY be to the Father, etc.

39 The Ascension Eve.   40 The Ascension Day.
41 Lord's Day Next after Ascension.—

Introd. Resp.   [Ps. xxiv, 9.]

LIFT up your heads, O Ye Gates !
Even lift them up, Ye everlasting Doors !—
And the King of Glory shall come in.

Special Morning Hymn, 179 [L.M. omit 6th.]—Our Lord is risen from the dead—.

Special Evening Hymn, [L.M. From Sabbath Hymn Book, by permission.]

1 Lift up your heads, ye gates ! and wide
 Your everlasting doors display ;
 Ye angel-guards, like flames divide,
  And give the King of glory way.

3 Lift up your heads, ye gates ! and high
 Your everlasting portals heave ;
 Welcome the King of Glory nigh :
  Him must the heaven of heavens receive.

2 Who is the King of glory ?—He,
 The Lord, omnipotent to save ;
 Whose own right arm, in victory,
  Led captive Death, and spoiled the grave.

4 Who is the King of Glory ?—who ?
 The Lord of hosts ; behold His name :
 The kingdom, power, and honor due,
  Yield Him, ye saints, with glad acclaim !

5 To FATHER, Son, and Holy Ghost,
 Thou God, Whom Earth and Heaven adore.
 Be Glory as it was of old,
 Is now, and shall be evermore !

Special Chant.   [Ps. xxiv, 5-10 ; xlvii, 1, 2, 5, &c.]

LIFT up your heads! O Ye Gates !
And be ye lift up, ye Everlasting Doors !
And the King of Glory shall come in.

WHO is this King of Glory ?
The Lord, strong and mighty,
The Lord mighty in battle.

LIFT up your heads ! O Ye Gates !
Even lift them up, Ye Everlasting Doors !
And the King of Glory shall come in.

WHO is this King of Glory ?
The Lord of Hosts, He is the King of Glory.

O CLAP your hands all ye people !
Shout unto God with the voice of triumph !
For the Lord Most High is terrible :
He is a great King over all the Earth.

GOD is gone up with a shout,
The Lord with the sound of a trumpet.
God reigneth over the heathen :
God sitteth upon the Throne of His holiness.—

Doxology of David (p. 52).

Gloria Patri.

---

42 𝕿𝖍𝖊 𝕻𝖊𝖓𝖙𝖊𝖈𝖔𝖘𝖙 𝕰𝖛𝖊. 43 𝕿𝖍𝖊 𝕻𝖊𝖓𝖙𝖊𝖈𝖔𝖘𝖙 𝕯𝖆𝖞. 44 𝕷𝖔𝖗𝖉'𝖘 𝕯𝖆𝖞 𝕹𝖊𝖝𝖙 𝖆𝖋𝖙𝖊𝖗 𝕻𝖊𝖓𝖙𝖊𝖈𝖔𝖘𝖙.
61 𝕸𝖎𝖉 𝕾𝖚𝖒𝖒𝖊𝖗 𝕯𝖆𝖞. 52 𝕸𝖎𝖉 𝕾𝖚𝖒𝖒𝖊𝖗 𝕷𝖔𝖗𝖉'𝖘 𝕯𝖆𝖞.

Introd. Resp. [Ps. l, 1, 2.]

THE Mighty God, even the Lord, hath spoken,
And called the Earth from the rising of the Sun unto the going
down thereof.
Out of Zion the Perfection of beauty, God hath shined.

Special Morning Hymn, 205 [L.M.]—Come, O Creator Spirit Blest !—
Special Evening Hymn, 222 [7s. Omit 5th stanza.]—Holy Spirit ! Lord of light !—

66 𝕷𝖔𝖗𝖉'𝖘 𝕯𝖆𝖞 𝕱𝖎𝖗𝖘𝖙 𝖎𝖓 𝕮𝖍𝖚𝖗𝖈𝖍 𝕾𝖊𝖆𝖘𝖔𝖓. 71 𝕷𝖔𝖗𝖉'𝖘 𝕯𝖆𝖞 𝕾𝖎𝖝𝖙𝖍 𝖎𝖓 𝕮𝖍𝖚𝖗𝖈𝖍 𝕾𝖊𝖆𝖘𝖔𝖓.

Introd. Resp. [Ps. cxxii, 1. 2.]

I WAS glad when they said unto Me—
Let Us go into the House of the Lord !
Our feet shall stand within thy gates, O Jerusalem !

Special Morning Hymn, 668 [L.M.]—Eternal Father ! Thou hast said—.
Special Evening Hymn, 656 [7s & 6s]—Hail to the Lord's anointed—.

Special Chant (for all the above days).

[Ps. xlviii. 1-3, 9-14.]

¹ GREAT | is the | Lord !
  And | greatly | to be | praised
² In the City | of our | God,
  In the | mountain | of His | holiness.
³ Beautiful for | situ- | ation,
  The joy of the whole | Earth, is | Mount | Zion,
⁴ The City of the | Great | King.
  God is known in her | palaces ˙ for | a | Refuge.

⁵ WE have thought of Thy loving kindness, | O | God !
  In the | midst of· | Thy | temple.

⁶ According to Thy | Name, O | God !
    So is Thy praise | un-to the | ends ˙ of the | Earth.
⁷ Thy right hand is | full of | righteousness
    Let Mount | Zi- | on re- | joice !
⁸ Let the daughters of | Judah ˙ be | glad,
    Be- | cause | of Thy | judgments.

⁹ WALK a- | bout | Zion,
    And go | round a- | bout | her :
¹⁰ Tell the | towers ˙ there- | of :
    Mark ye | well | her | bulwarks :
¹¹ Consider | her | palaces ;
    That ye may tell it to the | gener- | ation | following.
¹² For this God is our God for | ever ˙ and | ever :
    He will be our | Guide ˙ even | unto | death.—

¹³,¹⁴ GLORY be to the Father, etc.

---

77 **Cibil Thanksgibing Day.**—Any extraordinary Thanksgiving Service.—

Introd. Resp.   [Rev. xix, 1, 3, 4.]

ALLELUIA !
Salvation, and Glory, and Honor, and Power, unto the Lord
    our God !
Alleluia !—AMEN !

Special Hymn, 837 [L.M. Omit / 4th stanza.]—Eternal source of every joy !—

Special Chant.   [Ps. cxlvii, 1, 5, 7, 8, 12-16, 17, 19.]

¹ PRAISE | Ye the | Lord !
    For it is good to sing | praises | unto ˙ our | God :
² Great is our Lord, and of | great | power :
    His under- | stand- | ing is | infinite.

³ SING unto the Lord with | thanks- | giving !
    Who covereth the | heaven | with | clouds,
⁴ Who prepareth | rain ˙ for the | Earth,
    Who maketh grass to | grow up- | on the | mountains.

⁵ PRAISE the Lord, | O Je- | rusalem !
    Praise thy | God, | O | Zion !

⁶ For He hath strengthened the | bars * of thy | gates,
He hath blessed thy | children * with- | in ¦ thee.

⁷ He maketh peace | in thy | borders,
And filleth thee with the | finest | of the | wheat.

⁸ He sendeth forth His commandment | upon | Earth,
His | word * runneth | very | swiftly.

⁹ He giveth | snow like | wool :
Who can | stand be- | fore His | cold ?

¹⁰ He showeth His | word * unto | Jacob,
His statutes and His | judgments | unto | Israel.—

Doxology of David (p. 52).

Gloria Patri.

Christian Doxologies.

In these, the endeavor has been made, by altering old forms, and supplying new ones, to secure not only *calls* to praise, but direct *ascriptions* of praise to God as Father, Son, and Holy Ghost.

L. M.

To FATHER, Son, and Holy Ghost,
Thou God, Whom Earth and Heaven adore,
Be Glory, as it was of old,
Is now, and shall be evermore !

L. M.

GLORY to Thee, O God, most High !
Father, We praise Thy majesty !
The Son, the Spirit, We adore,
One Godhead, blest for evermore !

C. M.

To FATHER, Son, and Holy Ghost,
Thou God, Whom We adore,
Be Glory as it was, is now,
And shall be evermore !

S. M.

THE Father and the Son
And Spirit we adore;
We praise, We bless, We worship Thee,
One God for evermore !

7s.

THEE, Eternal God, Most High !
Thee We laud and magnify !
Praising with the heavenly host,
Father, Son, and Holy Ghost !

8s & 7s.

FATHER ! unto Thee be given,
With the Son, and Spirit, praise !
Mighty God ! Let Earth and Heaven
Worship Thee through endless days !

8s & 7s.   *Double.*

LORD ! Thy glorious Name confessing,
We take up the Angel's cry—
Holy ! Holy ! Holy !—blessing
Thee, the Lord our God Most High !
Father ! unto Thee be given,
With the Son, and Spirit, praise !
Mighty God ! Let Earth and Heaven
Worship Thee through endless days !

7s & 6s.   *Double.*

FATHER ! to Thee be praises !
And to Thine Only Son !
The Heaven its anthem raises
While ceaseless ages run :
Thy Holy Spirit, blessing—
Angels and saints adore :
Thee, Mighty Lord ! confessing—
One God for evermore !

10s & 11s.

O FATHER Almighty, to Thee be addressed,
With Christ and the Spirit, one God ever blest,
All glory and worship from Earth and from Heaven.
As was, and is now, and shall ever be given !

S P. M.

To THY high majesty,
Eternal praises be,
From Earth and all the Heavenly host !—
Thou God Whom We adore
Now and for evermore :
The Father, Son, and Holy Ghost !